One
Page
Talent
Management

One Page Talent Management

Eliminating Complexity, Adding Value

MARC EFFRON + MIRIAM ORT

Harvard Business Press

Boston, Massachusetts

Library of Congress Cataloging-in-Publication Data

Effron, Marc.
One page talent management : eliminating complexity, adding value / Marc Effron and Miriam Ort.
    p. cm.
ISBN 978-1-4221-6673-4 (hbk. : alk. paper)
1. Manpower planning. 2. Human capital—Management. 3. Performance. 4. Personnel management. I. Ort, Miriam. II. Title.
HF5549.5.M3E34 2010
658.3'01—dc22

                                            2009053360

The paper used in this publication meets the requirements of the American National Standard for Permanence of Paper for Publications and Documents in Libraries and Archives Z39.48-1992.

CONTENTS

PREFACE

In early 2006, when we began developing the approach that forms the basis of this book, setting a framework for talent management design was nowhere on our agenda. Our focus was completely practical. We had been asked to build and implement new talent management practices to support the turnaround of a $9 billion consumer products company. The company needed the practices quickly. It had to demonstrate results in a short time. What we delivered deviated from the more traditional views of how human resource (HR) and talent management practices should look and function. We had consciously worked to remove any extra features and complexity, while simultaneously trying to add value into each to make the practices more effective.

Although we were confident that these easier, value-adding practices would deliver superior results, early, reliable measures of our approach were still months away. However, in May 2007, a brief feature in the *New Yorker* gave us a little reassurance that we were onto something. The article described the problem of "feature creep"—the addition of tens or even hundreds of features to electronic devices like digital cameras. It said that engineers who were motivated to create cool, but not necessarily usable, technology were adding these extra features. At the other end of the product chain were consumers who were suffering from "feature fatigue," utterly confused about how to operate their devices due to the numerous options. A study on the topic showed that when given the choice, consumers most frequently selected the camera with the most features. However, when asked to use the camera they had selected, they quickly became frustrated and ultimately settled for a simpler design.[1] In short, while complexity was easy to make, market, and sell, complexity did not work.

We read that article and felt it was a perfect analogy for our design approach. The myriad options available in typical HR practices were the same as in a complicated camera—cool, but adding marginal value and complicating the overall experience. Rather than designing the typical camera, we had focused on making it usable, removing ten features but adding in autofocus so the user could achieve the core objective of taking better pictures. Complexity eliminated, value added.

How We Got Here

That design approach and this book describing it results from a culmination of experiences rather than a blinding flash of inspiration. For Marc, the foundational experience occurred when he was a young political consultant in Southern California using a simple approach to help small-town water board, school board, and city council candidates win elections. The consulting firm he worked for believed that candidates won elections for two reasons only—high personal trust and high name recognition. It felt that a candidate should focus exclusively on maximizing those two factors and had developed a consulting approach to achieve that.

As a candidates' consultant, Marc would tell them exactly how to increase personal trust and name recognition, with every instruction focusing on a few, powerful levers for victory. Among other things, they would learn the size, color, and copy for their campaign signs (three feet by five feet, blue letters on white background, name and position only) and get the exact script they were to use when talking to voters. All this advice was captured in a twenty-page booklet he gave to candidates.

What activities were the candidates prohibited from? Anything that wasn't proven to work, including distributing potholders, running radio ads, and hosting or attending wine and cheese parties. The victory rate for Marc's candidates was about mid 80 percent. The candidates learned two clear lessons—what is simple works, and avoid distractions.

After a business school career change, for the next twenty years, Marc had broad exposure through corporate and consulting experiences to what worked and did not work in growing talent. As the leadership consulting practice leader for Hewitt Associates, one of the world's largest HR consultancies, Marc saw what made talent practices work in hundreds of organizations worldwide. And, from more than three years of the *Top Companies for Leaders Study* that he created in 2001, he was able to extract from the data of more than six hundred companies, the three key elements that allowed them to consistently grow great talent.[2] One of those elements was that companies that consistently produced great earnings and great talent did not have the most sophisticated or most complex talent processes. Instead, they had processes that fit their culture, were relatively simple, and were flawlessly executed.

Marc started with Avon Products in late 2005, just prior to the launch of its turnaround effort. He sought an opportunity to approach talent management in a new way, applying the sum of his experiences, and this was it. Miriam Ort was a manager on his talent management team and a five-year Avon veteran. In the years leading up to Avon's turnaround efforts, she had seen an organization flush with cash and touting double-digit growth that was unable to take advantage of several appealing acquisitions due to limited bench. At the same time, the organization had rolled out a number of new talent practices, some even written up as best practices. Somehow, the beautifully designed and well-benchmarked processes were not translating into the bottom-line talent depth Avon so desperately needed. This lesson underscored the need for the usable, outcome-oriented processes that were later embodied in our approach.

As we worked to redesign Avon's talent practices, our combined experiences gave us a strong point of view about how talent should be grown. The result was a structured approach and philosophy for building talent that we call One Page Talent Management (OPTM).

One Page Talent Management

OPTM is a radical departure from typical corporate talent development processes. Its goal is straightforward—increase talent depth and quality in the simplest, easiest way possible. We believe that can be accomplished only by creating the shortest path from the proven behavioral science to the desired business outcome. This book details exactly how to do that by starting with the science, eliminating complexity, and adding value to each process. We also describe how to maximize the effectiveness of each process by making it transparent and ensuring accountability for its execution.

Our approach is not a set of best practices, and we do not believe that there is one best version of any talent process. Although we provide an example in each chapter of what an OPTM-inspired process could look like, you might follow our design process and reach a completely different result. We suggest that, given that your business challenges, leaders, and values are likely different from ours, your results *should not* look like the generic examples we present.

About the Book

We believe that successful companies are a consequence of great leaders and that their success has positive results for their communities and society as a whole. More successful companies are more innovative and create more jobs, more tax revenue, more economic stability, and a plethora of other benefits. When those great companies produce even more great leaders, it becomes a virtuous cycle. However, current research suggests that this is not happening. There is a dearth of talent, and the processes to build more have not yielded results. The solutions we suggest are meant to restart and accelerate talent growth in all companies.

What We Cover, What We Don't

Although there are many factors that influence how talent is grown, we include the most powerful, repeatable processes that create successful talent. We include talent reviews and competencies because they underlie your ability to assess talent quality and depth, and to drive changes where needed. We also include performance management, 360-degree feedback, and engagement because they create high-performing leaders and organizations that achieve superior business results.

We are guided by the findings from the New Talent Management Network's (NTMN) annual talent management report. NTMN (www.newtmn.com) is an organization of more than sixteen hundred talent management leaders focused on increasing the profession's impact and influence. In 2007, Marc founded the nonprofit organization, which has since grown to the largest of its type. Its research shows that companies define talent management largely as consisting of the practices we mentioned earlier.

NTMN has found that corporate talent management groups most frequently manage recurring processes designed to grow talent, like succession planning and high-potential identification, while less frequently engaging in practices like team interventions and change management. Talent acquisition responsibilities were included in talent management groups less than 50 percent of the time, and training about 40 percent.[3] Although we do not intend to engage in the highly debated question about the parameters of talent management as a function or field, we consciously choose to focus on the areas where talent-oriented practitioners seem to be prioritizing their resources.

Our Research and Examples

We reviewed literally hundreds of original academic papers to ensure that our book was thoroughly grounded in the core behavioral and organizational science. When we use the term "core science", our primary focus is academic research—peer reviewed and published. Consulting firms and others also conduct interesting and helpful research, but the empirical and transparent nature of the academic research provides a belt-and-suspenders level of confidence that we feel is needed when making talent management decisions. We present both academic and consulting research throughout the book, so you can decide which sources seem most valid to you. In each chapter, we describe what this science says about how to drive behaviors and show how it supports each OPTM design.

While most companies are still battling complex, bureaucratic talent processes, we were fortunate to find a few others using a "one page" approach in at least parts of their talent processes. You will read examples from perennially successful companies like American Express, General Mills, PepsiCo, Avon Products, and IBM.

We also gained insight on the state of talent management from interviews with a number of experienced and highly respected human resource executives, talent management practitioners, and consultants in this field. The HR executives included Kevin Cox at American Express, Lucien Alziari at Avon Products, and P. V. Ramana Murthy at Coca-Cola (India). Each has led successful transformations of talent management in their organizations.

The talent management practitioners included Allan Church at PepsiCo; Mary Eckenrod at Research In Motion; Rachel Lee at American Express; Mike Markovits at IBM; Jim Shanley, formerly at Bank of America; and Kevin Wilde at General Mills. These deeply experienced and highly respected practitioners have built talent management systems that consistently contribute to strong business results in their organizations.

Helping us to gain a broad perspective of talent management practices worldwide were DeAnne Aguirre, a senior partner and organizational change expert at Booz & Co.; John Gibbons who leads the research practice for The Conference Board; Dr. Robert Lefton and his team at Psychological Associates; and N. S. Rajan, partner, human capital and global leader, HR Advisory at Ernst & Young and also head of India's Human Resource Development Network. Their combined experiences and wisdom are integrated throughout the book.

Our Thanks

Our book represents the collective experiences, influences, and challenges we have had. We would jointly like to thank everyone who provided input into our manuscript: DeAnne Aguirre, Lucien Alziari, Anne Beatty, Melinda Bramley, Allan Church, Kevin Cox, Mary Eckenrod, Bill Farmer, John Gibbons, Rachel Lee, Dr. Robert Lefton, Mike Markovits, P. V. Ramana Murthy, Macaire Pace, Jason Pegg, N. S. Rajan, Jim Shanley, Lauren Tate, and Kevin Wilde. This book would not have been possible without the support and guidance of Melinda Merino, our editor at Harvard Business Press. Melinda first suggested that we turn our "one page" concept into a book and then expertly guided us through the editorial process. Her staff at HBP were unfailing helpful, and we want to extend a special thank you to Courtney Schinke for her editorial support and Stephani Finks for designing a wonderful book jacket.

Thoughts from Marc: This book draws on the insights, support, and experiences provided by many people during my career. While there isn't room to thank all of you personally, please know that I deeply appreciate the counsel, direction, challenges, and encouragement that you have given me. My deepest thanks go to Marshall Goldsmith, whose philosophy and approach inspired OPTM and who has had an immeasurably positive impact on my work and personal life. In addition to cocreating the OPTM concept, Miriam Ort has been the ideal writing partner, bringing balance, insight, structure, and inspiration where there was none. And to my wife Michelle, who provided wonderful support, put up with the late hours, and didn't see me on any Sundays in 2009, thank you.

Thoughts from Miriam: My work on this book is a reflection of the many people who have taken the time to mentor and support me throughout the years. First and foremost, to my coauthor, Marc Effron: it has been a privilege to partner on the development of One Page Talent Management, both as a concept and a book. Thank you for your coaching, wisdom, mentorship, and for everything you have taught me about talent management. Lucien Alziari provided me with the opportunity to get involved with much of the work that contributed to this book, and the sponsorship to succeed.

For taking a bet on me, and for your ongoing commitment to my development—thank you. And every day, colleagues, clients, and mentors continue to influence, challenge, and inspire me. While that list is too long to include here, please accept my sincerest appreciation.

To my family, who is always there cheering me on, forgiving my workaholism, and helping me keep my priorities straight: I am so very fortunate to have you. And finally, a heartfelt thank you to my husband Eli, whose flexibility, understanding, and support for my work have made all the difference.

1

One Page Talent Management

A highly respected business journal has recently published an article proving that when a CEO makes and serves a cake to his employees, it causes huge increases in employee engagement {humor us}. Two CEOs read the article, believe the findings, and commit to making a cake for their staff. They each ask their talent management leader to design a process that will produce a suitable cake.

In Company 1, the talent leader is excited about this challenge. His goal is to design a plan that will allow the CEO to make a world-class cake. He starts by benchmarking the best cakes in the best companies around the globe and consulting with renowned bakers. He takes this knowledge and everything he has ever learned about cake making and designs a detailed cake-making plan. When followed correctly, his plan will produce a five-tiered cake with flowers of multicolored frosting cascading from layer to layer, intricate icing designs, a working fountain of melted chocolate, and a rich butter-cream filling flavored with imported Madagascar vanilla.

When his plan is finished, the proud talent leader hands the CEO a 73-page instruction manual, 124 different ingredients, and 7 pans.

This, he tells her, will produce a world-class cake with less than 100 hours of effort. The CEO politely thanks the talent leader but wonders how she can ever make this cake. She's committed to making a cake, but she simply can't justify the time and energy required to make this one. When she asks the talent leader if there's another way, he repeats that this is a great cake-making plan—in fact, GE uses a very similar plan to make its cakes. The busy CEO never finds the time to make that cake, and without cake her staff's engagement decreases and the company's performance declines.

At Company 2, the talent management leader is equally committed to the goal. She understands that the CEO has great intentions but no expertise in cake making and little time to learn. Her goal is to develop a solution that will meet the CEO's goal— employees eat cake and become engaged. She knows that she has to make the process as easy and understandable as possible if her busy CEO is going to use it. Although she's quite competent in making cakes, she starts by reviewing the science behind making a great cake to ensure she's applying the fundamentals correctly. Her research reminds her that only six ingredients are required to make a cake, and she realizes that the process might be easier than she had thought. (On a benchmarking visit to Company 1, she had seen the cake design proposed by its talent leader and, while she admired the intricate detailing and cake "bling," she didn't think they supported the core goal. She decided not to include those extras in her cake design.)

Finally, she realizes that while her basic recipe simplifies the steps involved in making the cake, she can add even more value. She mixes together the dry ingredients to create a cake mix, greatly reducing both the time the CEO will need to spend making the cake and the chance for error. She gives it to the CEO with two eggs, a can of frosting, a pan, and a one page instruction sheet. She tells him that in one hour this simple process and few essential ingredients will make a nice cake that the employees will enjoy. The CEO sees that with little effort he'll be able to serve his employees cake, making them, him, and the talent leader happy. The client now values the talent leader, who gets invited to have a seat at the table and share the cake.

SOUND A LITTLE SILLY? Substitute "performance management" or "succession planning" for "making a cake." Does your organization resemble Company 1, with academically perfect talent-building processes that are both unusable and unused? Or are you closer to Company 2, building talent with lean, easy-to-use processes that are guaranteed to achieve results?

Recent research by McKinsey & Company, Boston Consulting Group, and Deloitte suggest the former.[1] Their studies confirm that organizations are unhappy with their ability to grow talent and are becoming increasingly frustrated as their talent needs become more severe. Outside their walls, they see a competitive environment in which winning requires top-quality talent, while inside those walls, they see millions spent on talent development with very few results. Line executives blame human resource (HR) groups for not delivering better leaders, while HR says those same executives talk a great game but do not deliver the necessary resources or commitment.

While this situation is challenging, it is also somewhat strange due to one key fact: we already know almost everything necessary to grow great talent. Sixty years of high-quality behavioral and industrial/organizational psychology research can help us understand how companies and employees can work best together. We understand the combination of job experiences, coaching, and formal training that is optimal for development. We know which talent practices have proven to be effective over time. In short, we already have nearly every answer needed to develop talent in our organizations.

Yet, there seems to be a gap between our knowledge of how to develop talent and our ability to actually do it. This is difficult to understand, given that most companies have an HR department and many larger companies have dedicated talent management or leadership development groups focused on precisely that task. So, if our organizations want to grow talent, know how to do it, and have the resources necessary to get it done, what is not working? More importantly, how can we fix it?

Four Barriers to Building Talent

Through our corporate and consulting experience, we have identified four talent-building barriers that organizations create for themselves and then regularly stumble over. These barriers explain why line executives' exhortations and HR's actions to build talent are not translating into increased talent quality and depth.

Creating Needless Complexity

When you consider the simple intent behind most talent processes, it can be challenging to understand why a line manager experiences so much complexity. A simple process like setting goals often becomes a multipage, headache-inducing exercise and in doing so puts a huge barrier in the way of increasing organizations' performance.

Where organizations go wrong is that they fail to balance complexity with value as they build these processes. It is not that the additional components layered on—from highly detailed competency models to the extra hundred questions on an engagement survey—are technically wrong. Many have sound behavioral science to support their inclusion. However, as each additional element is added, evaluating the trade-off between the complexity it brings to the *overall* process and the impact it will have on the original business objective is critical.

Adding No New Value

Talent management tools have not been designed to help managers make smarter decisions or to make their jobs easier. Managers often need to attend training sessions to learn how to use a talent tool or process or must rely on their HR manager or other expert to help them. When a manager receives an engagement survey report, can he quickly understand the business choices he should make because of it? The talent review process may differentiate the best talent from the rest, but do managers know how to use that information productively? In many organizations, managers have come to see talent management tools and processes as largely divorced from their day-to-day management challenges.

Neglecting the Science

As we mentioned earlier, HR and talent management can rely on a rich body of academic research to help inform the right decisions. Basic behavioral science (e.g., Ivan Pavlov's classic conditioning or B. F. Skinner's behavioral research) provided the foundation for the industrial and organizational psychology research (e.g., Victor Vroom's expectancy theory or Richard Hackman and Greg Oldham's job design) of the past fifty years that informs every modern talent practice, from 360-degree feedback to conducting performance reviews.

If companies would faithfully follow this science, they would find that it performs up to its billing. Their talent practices would work as the research suggests they should. If they do not understand or choose to ignore the science, companies will build talent practices using biases and assumptions and wonder why their talent problems are not going away.

Lacking Transparency and Accountability

Few managers enjoy having tough conversations with their employees. Giving feedback about subpar performance or explaining that a career goal will never be achieved significantly increases most managers' heart rates. But transparent conversations like these drive higher performance. Unfortunately, in too many companies, fear of the consequences or a genuine belief that employees do not need this level of clarity means talent practices are opaque.

It's also understandable that managers usually prioritize coaching, performance feedback, and creating development plans after activities that provide a more immediate benefit to their business. These talent practices are still important, however, and most organizations do not hold their managers accountable for executing them.

Designing a New Approach

In late 2005, finding a way to overcome these challenges dominated our thoughts. Marc was the recently appointed vice president of talent management for a $9 billion consumer packaged-goods company, and Miriam was a manager on his team. The company had started a major restructuring process that would require great talent to achieve its objectives and strong talent processes to sustain them. The organization was not utilizing the talent processes in place, which unfortunately felt like those in Company 1. Our charge was to make fundamental changes that would allow the company to quickly and easily identify the talent it had, deploy that talent in the most effective possible way, and rapidly develop critical capabilities. As an added twist, we had to build and implement these processes and show meaningful results in less than a year in order to support the turnaround.

Sitting at a conference table in our New York City office, we started to address our task with a blank sheet of paper. We knew that we had great latitude in what processes we proposed for performance management, talent reviews, and other talent practices. We also knew the somewhat depressing research on the effectiveness of those practices. We recognized that we had to find a better way.

Since little research existed about why talent practices succeeded in organizations, we asked ourselves what we knew to be true. We concluded that:

The science works. We knew that, thanks to legions of behavioral and industrial/organizational psychologists, how to change leaders' behaviors, grow their skills, align them with the business, and achieve almost any other desired organizational outcome was widely known. Although that research still required some translation into actual process designs, the raw material did, for the most part, exist.

Only implementation matters. Our experience (and a little common sense) told us that no matter how artful the design, a talent practice would work only if it was being used. Unfortunately, we had seen that many companies' talent practices were bureaucratic, complex, and time consuming, so managers either did not use them or made a minimum effort to comply.

Managers want to succeed. Line managers have challenging goals, and most welcome a talent tool or process that helps them to be successful. In our corporate and consulting experience, we had heard from managers worldwide that traditional talent practices from talent reviews to 360-degree feedback seemed designed to benefit HR, not to help the average manager.

Transparency and accountability guarantee results. We understood the noise caused in an organization when processes were not transparent. Eliminating that noise would make the processes more legitimate and likely to be used. We also understood that some managers would never elevate talent to the top of their agenda. For them, and for forgetful others, accountability for talent outcomes was required.

We were confident that if we used these truths to shape our talent practices, the results would be at least somewhat more effective than traditional talent processes and, we hoped, much more.

Our design process started by identifying the business's most urgent talent objectives. First, we needed to understand the quality and depth of the company's talent in order to ensure that we could make the right talent selection and investment decisions. Next we needed everyone in the organization aligned on the vital few goals and behaviors that would turn around the business. This alignment would accelerate progress toward those goals. Finally, we needed to raise engagement to the highest possible level to maximize every associate's performance.

We designed our solutions by faithfully applying our four truths. Since we knew the science worked, we researched what the core science found to be effective at driving individual and company performance, not how HR practices were typically designed. We knew that only implementation mattered, so we stripped complexity from existing processes and built new ones that balanced complexity with a commensurate amount of value. Our constant focus was on whether the most skeptical managers would find the process simple and valuable enough to use. Since we knew that transparency and accountability guaranteed results, we built these elements into every practice.

When we finished designing our processes, even we were surprised by the results. After accurately translating the research into practice, we were left with the simplest possible path from science to effective

Focus on the Business Objective: Creating Clear and Motivating Goals

When we wanted to set and communicate goals that would maximize performance, we examined the academic research on goal setting, not the best practices in performance management. In the research, we found four key concepts related to setting motivational goals— goals should be extremely challenging, in the employee's self-interest, few in number, and very specific. Along with those findings, we found research that disproved conventional goal-setting wisdom, including that participation in goal setting improves performance and that one scale is superior to another (and more that we detail in chapter 2).

In our goal-setting design, we included just those elements proven to work and left out everything without clear science to support it. The result was a model of OPTM applied to the performance management process. Our finished goal-setting form kept employees focused on the most important goals by allowing no more than four to be listed. Since the science did not indicate that anything else was needed, we included just two boxes per goal—the goal and the metric. A one page instruction sheet explained how to write goals that were challenging and in the employee's self-interest.

This new process—our first attempt to design on one page— yielded two benefits. The expected benefit was that participation in goal setting went from about 30 percent to above 90 percent. The unexpected benefit was that managers now understood that we had their best interests at heart, which gave us permission to continue our talent management transformation.

execution. Practices that managers had experienced as intensive, bureaucratic, time-consuming exercises had been reduced to one page, intuitive, business tools. When we applied this approach to our performance management process, for example, the result was a simple, one page form that managers quickly adopted. In every practice, the elements of complexity that could not justify their overall value to managers had fallen away.

Not only was complexity gone, but value had been added back. We could now turn complex HR data into valuable insights for managers. We could tell them exactly which actions would increase engagement in their group and by how much. We could highlight the most important behaviors for them to change, while avoiding the resistance that typically accompanies 360-degree feedback. We had found a way to turn the theoretical power of behavioral science into actual results.

Long-Term Performance Results

This is an appropriate time to ask whether this very untraditional approach actually delivered results. It is also a good time to briefly share our point of view on talent metrics, which, as you may now suspect, varies somewhat from traditional views. We are big fans of quantitatively measuring talent results and using the data to make decisions about talent. However, we believe that the best overall talent metric is the long-term performance of the business. Other talent metrics are interesting intermediate measures of process performance and, although helpful in measuring progress, do not measure the only talent outcome many shareholders and executives care about.

Long-term performance is also a good metric because, if you believe what the research indicates—that better leaders deliver better results—over time, better talent practices deliver better leaders who deliver better performance. Both the Top Companies for Leaders research and a number of academic studies provide ample proof.[2] In short, if talent management is working well, the company is much more likely to succeed. We also recognize that although talent is critically important, hundreds of other variables affect corporate performance. It would be wonderful if it were possible to draw a straight line from talent practices to specific business outcomes, but it is not.

For the work on talent management that we did in our company, we can point to corporate performance metrics and both quantitative and qualitative measures of process performance. During the three years after we implemented our OPTM processes, our organization was able to reduce administrative expenses by nearly 4 percent, increase revenue by more than 20 percent, increase profit margins by almost 50 percent, and was regularly cited by the media as a well-run organization.[3] These were certainly strong results, but can be considered even stronger because they were delivered during the worst economic crisis since the Great Depression.

At the process level, we worked to increase engagement, the power of talent reviews, and the effectiveness of performance management, among other efforts. Engagement increased 20 percent (30 percent among managers), and performance discussions took place for more than 90 percent of associates, up from less than 30 percent. The number of "ready now" successors for key roles increased by 25 percent, even though we aggressively increased the quality standards for talent each year. Our success rate for using coaching to change behaviors went from well below 50 percent to north of 90 percent. There are many more similar results that we could present.

Strangely, the qualitative measures actually seem more powerful than the quantitative ones. General managers thanked us for the new performance management process. That was certainly the first time in our careers we had ever heard that! The executive team praised the talent review process as the most effective in the company's history and said that better people decisions were being made faster because of it. Engagement was woven into the culture of the company. There were more qualified general managers available for key roles. We had moved a meaningful amount of talent who no longer fit out of the organization. Overall, these metrics seemed a much better measure of success than anything quantitative.

Can we claim that everything that went well with talent was because of our processes? Of course not. It would be impossible to separate out the effects of new executive team members, adjusted compensation structures, and all the other variables that might have had an impact on talent outcomes. Still, at the end of four years, we felt comfortable claiming that our approach was more effective than typical talent process and, very likely, quite a bit more.

The Added Benefits of Simplification

It Gets Even Better

If having talent practices that allow you to build better leaders faster is not enough to convince you that OPTM is the right approach, a few other benefits are worth considering.

Line managers get a free week. If you transform talent practices, managers will get back at least forty hours a year compared to what they are spending now on current talent practices. Processes that used to take an hour per employee will take as little as fifteen minutes.

The design process is faster. Although it might seem intuitive, simpler processes take much less time to create. Weeks, not months, are needed to design and implement talent practices. A faster design cycle means you will start building better leaders, even faster. It also means that you can get feedback more quickly on which parts of the design need adjustment, make fast changes, and re-release the new process in record time.

Processes are cheaper to design. Less complex processes do not require as much consulting time, as many benchmarking trips, or other costs traditionally associated with the design process. Given the $50,000 to $500,000 you can spend designing and implementing more traditional talent practices, OPTM starts to look even more compelling.

HR earns the right to do more. A simple, effective process quickly wins the loyalty of managers and executives. They will be much more receptive to your next recommendation if your last one proved its effectiveness.

One Page Talent Management

Shortly after we began implementing these practices, we were invited to speak to a leading HR group about the talent management changes our company was making. Needing a clever title for the presentation, we coined "One Page Talent Management." We now use the term to define the integration of behavioral science, simplicity, accountability, and transparency into practices that accelerate the development of talent.

As we mentioned in the preface, we use OPTM both figuratively and literally. As an integrating concept, it stands for the addition of value and removal of complexity from talent practices. At the most practical level, it suggests a design discipline for creating these practices and a metric for evaluating their design. We do not expect that the key form or process for every talent practice can be reduced to one page, but we believe that aspiration forces an entirely new way of thinking about process design. Most importantly, we consider the OPTM approach to be a superior way to grow better leaders faster.

Since our experience with this new approach at Avon, we have presented this concept to thousands of HR leaders around the world, helped other companies to develop their own OPTM processes, and learned from seeing the full cycle of design, implementation, and evaluation. Through those experiences, we have refined a design process that will allow you to successfully implement OPTM in your organization.

In the next seven chapters, we describe the fundamental science that underlies each talent practice and how to use it to design simple and value-added processes that work. We also tell you how to overcome the objections you may hear from HR peers, consultants, academics, and others who have a different view of how companies should develop their talent. Let's get started.

The OPTM Design Steps

Based on the four truths we described earlier, we have created a straightforward, three-step process for designing OPTM processes.

Step 1. Start with the science.

Step 2. Eliminate complexity, add value.

Step 3. Create transparency and accountability.

Step 1. Start with the Science

Thousands of articles published during the past fifty years tell us why people and organizations behave as they do. From increasing employee satisfaction to building effective teams, we largely understand which levers to push or pull to get the optimal results. With the right answers readily available, the science seems like the logical place to start when creating talent practices.

The first step in the OPTM design process is to understand your business objectives and how the core behavioral and organizational science can help the company achieve them. For example, if the business objective is to increase sales in China, ask yourself what levers will make that happen? More motivational goals? Then what does the science say makes a goal motivational? Increased commitment? So what does commitment mean and what are the most significant drivers of it? By diagnosing the underlying issues at a more granular level, you will be better able to apply the core science as a solution.

That process may seem very basic, but it is often where HR departments stumble. When asked to solve business problems, too often the answers are presented as HR programs—better performance management or more training. By thinking about how to apply the core science to solve the underlying business issue, you will have taken the first step in successful OPTM design. To help you start with the science, we have summarized the key research findings that apply to each talent practice. In each chapter, we include the findings that are most conclusively proven and that have the most impact on process design. We have highlighted where researchers disagree on important points, and mentioned where there is a strongly held minority opinion as well. Our summaries cannot do justice to the breadth of information in the original articles, so if you have questions, we encourage you to dig into the original material.

Step 2. Eliminate Complexity, Add Value

Because talent practices work only if they are implemented, ensuring successful implementation must be the primary goal. By eliminating complexity and adding value, we help convince managers that these simple, easy-to-use practices will help them manage better with less effort. Although they stem from different truths, we have integrated eliminating complexity and adding value in Step 2 because they happen concurrently in the actual design process.

FIGURE 1-1

The Value-Complexity Curve

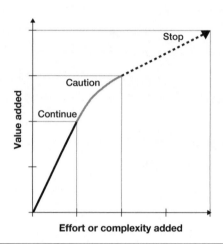

The key to Step 2 is to create a process that balances the complexity that managers experience in a process with the value they feel they derive from it. The OPTM process uses the Value-Complexity Curve (see figure 1-1) to help you maintain that balance during process design. It is a helpful way to ensure that you are not just eliminating complexity but that you are also finding ways to increase the value of the process for the manager.

Eliminating Complexity. Start the design process with a blank sheet of paper and try to put aside for the moment what you have heard is the right way to address talent challenges. Focus instead on solving the business objective. We have found the most effective design process involves taking small, incremental steps toward our goal, weighing the value-complexity trade-off at each step. For example, if your objective were to increase sales in China by creating more motivational goals, you would ask yourself what element of the goal-setting process would add more value than complexity? If your answer were, "Each manager could tell his or her staff people what their goals are," that would be both true to the science and would add more value than complexity. You would then look for other steps that would add more value while maintaining the balance with complexity. Maybe the manager could specify a clear metric for each goal that is backed by the science and would add more value than complexity both on its own and when combined with the first step.

As pedantic as it may seem, progressing this way guarantees that you evaluate the value-complexity trade-off for every single element and combination of elements. You should proceed this way until you start to see the value-complexity relationship begin to level, at which point you should become more cautious about adding new elements. Would adding individual goal weighting add more value than complexity? Probably not. Would including competencies in the goal significantly affect the outcome? No. What about something that reinforced important behaviors? Yes. When you reach the point at which no additional element adds more value than complexity, you

Iterations, Not Perfection

Although designing a perfect process on the first attempt is a wonderful goal, it is also completely unrealistic. We support an iterative process of input, design, test, and repeat, in which you roll out a new practice and transparently communicate that you will be gathering user feedback over time and modifying it to meet the users' needs. The key here is that the changes should be small adjustments to fine-tune the process, not a new design each year. The changes should also be meaningful enough to pass the value-complexity test: does making the change add enough value to justify the disruption of a new label, scale, and so on? This means the first attempt must still be very good, but you do not delay rolling out a new practice because it is not yet perfect.

are done. You will be amazed to see how many elements of traditional talent practices will have fallen away during this process. Elements that seemed to add value on their own often do not prove their incremental value as part of the overall process.

While you might expect that every design process would naturally seek a value-complexity balance, our experience is that what is commonly accepted as the right way is often tilted toward complexity. Even if the complexity is academically proven to add value, the challenge is to prove that it adds enough value to justify the additional complexity.

Another recommendation for eliminating complexity is to use the least amount of information needed to make the right decision. How many questions need to be on the 360-degree survey or engagement questionnaire to provide enough information to make the right decision? How many competencies are needed to align managers with the organization's goals and values? Be sure the standards you use to create processes are not the same used for publishing an academic paper. You want enough information to have confidence that you are taking the right action on the data, but no more than that.

Adding Value. If removing complexity from a talent process helps to ensure that the manager uses it, adding value helps ensure he or she uses it the right way. As you work through each design step, you should try to add value to each component. Adding value can mean making the process easier to use, pre-analyzing data for a manager, or narrowing a manager's choices of actions to the correct few. Can you analyze data for managers that they would otherwise have to evaluate themselves? Can you narrow the range of choices a manager has to make, eliminating in advance clearly inferior ones? There are more opportunities to add value to data-intensive processes or those that produce results requiring a manager's interpretation, like an engagement survey.

American Express: A One Page Response to Challenging Times

As the economic crisis worsened in late 2008, financial services firms were driven to reevaluate every dollar spent on talent management. American Express tasked the HR team with maintaining the company's historically strong focus on engagement in a resource-constrained environment. HR's response was a true model of OPTM.

Kevin Cox, executive vice president of HR, refocused his team on the core business objective previously served by the engagement survey—to identify and address underlying employee issues. The team knew that the survey was one way, but not the only one, to achieve that goal. Amex's talent development leaders challenged themselves to find the simplest (and cheapest) way to identify and address employee issues.

Their solution—the Employee Pulse Process—included "listening posts" (e.g., skip-level meetings, focus groups, questionnaires) to identify key issues, line-HR partnerships to understand the root causes, and leadership accountability to implement solutions. During 2008 and 2009, the new process helped executives improve the success of a new relationship management model, increase the frontline managers' ability to reach collection targets, and understand the ability of directors to lead through change, among other successes.

According to Rachel Lee, vice president, talent development and organizational capabilities, who helped create the Employee Pulse Process, "Our job was to get into the thick of the change, do a temperature check, and quickly get the leader findings they could act on." What did the leader see? A one page summary of the findings and a start, stop, continue model for moving forward.

Step 3. Create Transparency and Accountability

Although simplicity and adding value yield talent systems that are quick, effective, and easy to use, adding transparency and accountability will increase their power fivefold.

Transparency. We define transparency as the amount of information shared about a process and its results, and with whom that information is shared. To make any talent process truly effective, we suggest near total transparency as a starting point. Examples of transparency include telling leaders the results of discussions about performance and potential, sharing 360-degree feedback results openly, informing high potentials of their status, and other actions that scare the heck out of many HR and line leaders.

The argument for more transparency is overwhelming, and the argument against it is often based on irrational fear. American Express's Rachel Lee states it another way, "Why is it that total transparency in finance is good business but the same doesn't apply on the people side?" (See table 1-1 for a few examples of transparent actions.)

Transparency can turbocharge OPTM. Let's say you have developed a great OPTM version of a 360-degree assessment process that is both simple and adds value. Because of this new process, it is now fast and easy to participate in the new 360, and the report is focused and easy to understand. Your general managers take the 360, and it provides helpful insights.

At the end of the year, you have a job opening for a general manager in Antarctica, and you are considering two candidates for the job. It is a sensitive role, and you need someone who can quickly assimilate with the local staff, make major changes in the short term, and meet a variety of other challenges. Wouldn't you like to see a thorough, candid report on the candidates? Transparency in this situation would allow you to see that report, discuss the results with the general manager's future boss, and make a fact-based decision. Lack of transparency could lead to a very expensive mistake.

We understand that transparency can be difficult to achieve even in organizations with otherwise strong talent practices. A colleague at a well-respected company recently told us about the invitation

TABLE 1-1

Example of Transparent Action

Tell high potentials that they are high potentials

Fear-based reason not to be transparent	Reasons for transparency
They will leave if they find out they are that good. Keeping them in the dark is safer.	If you do not tell them they are high potential, a headhunter will be happy to tell them, and their next company will be happy to treat them like one. Besides, they already know (and they wonder why you have not told them!).
Knowing they are high potential will go to their heads and breed a sense of entitlement. Potential is based on one point in time; what if that designation changes?	As long as you clearly communicate to high potentials that it is not a permanent status, they will understand it is something they need to keep earning. If they no longer are high potential, it is better to tell them than to wait for frustration to set in when they notice their career trajectory slowing down.
Everyone else will be discouraged if some leaders are treated differently. It will destroy morale.	As long as you have accurately identified the high potentials, their coworkers will have been aware of their capability well before the formal decision. They will not be unhappy that others are considered high potential if they are being treated fairly as well. Those who thought they were high potential but are not will not be happy. It is better they find out now when they still have a chance to consider other options.

list for the company's meeting for high-potentials. On the list were managers who were obviously high potential and those who clearly were not, but who were invited for political reasons. To ensure that no one was misled by the list, the company also maintained a separate "shadow" list of the true high potentials.

Accountability. In an ideal world, the simple and easy-to-use processes of OPTM would be enough to convince managers to conduct talent reviews, give performance feedback, and get development plans done on time. In reality, busy managers may not always make the time or have the inclination to finish these tasks. Accountability is a necessary ingredient to ensure that the great potential of OPTM is not wasted. Although accountability for results is absent from most talent development practices, adding it can be quite simple. You can use peer pressure, corporate culture, compensation, and many other levers to enforce accountability for growing talent.

Let's add accountability into the 360-degree example discussed earlier. We now have useful behavioral data that can help us make smarter talent decisions, but how do we take this information and improve the employee's behavior? One step is to make the manager accountable for following up with the employee to identify the one behavior that he will change because of the results. We could require that this one behavior become part of the employee's one page development plan. The CEO or unit leader would assign accountability here, and HR would check on it.

You may think accountability can be driven only by the promise of cash or by withholding cash. Money can certainly help focus attention, but only so many goals can be tied to monetary rewards before the financial impact of each goal is relatively meaningless. There are many other ways of holding leaders accountable for actions and behaviors. We discuss these in more detail in each chapter. (See table 1-2 for a few examples.)

Our discussion of accountability and transparency should not distract you from a core belief in OPTM—that managers are accountable for their talent and should not need extra motivation in that area. We believe that managers' two primary responsibilities are to deliver business results and grow their talent. They are responsible for delivering praise and correcting people, actively developing them, and making the tough decisions about who must leave the organization. They are responsible for being transparent with their employees about their performance and potential to advance. Any lack of transparency steals from employees their ability to own and manage their careers effectively. No manager has that right.

TABLE 1-2

Examples of Accountability Actions

Accountability action	Example
Employee-driven upward	Tell employees that their managers are responsible to complete an activity (e.g., create a development plan), in a certain way (meet individually with each employee) by a certain date. Let the employees know that if this has not occurred, they should ask their manager and, if not satisfied with the response, their local HR leader.
Name and shame	You have not completed your performance reviews on time? Start with a reminder from their manager, then the next highest manager. If no response, share the list in staff meetings or post the list of culprits on the intranet or another very public place in the organization.
Create some competition	For any metric that is common across the organization (e.g., engagement survey scores), list the metric by manager and rank from top to bottom. Broadly communicate the results.
Measure in performance goals	What gets measured gets done. Almost any talent management activity can be tracked and measured. Identify which talent outcomes are most important and include quantitatively measured results in managers' performance goals.

OPTM Underlying Beliefs

We are confident that if you follow the OPTM design principles, you will have process designs that are simpler, more valuable, and much more likely to achieve business goals. The design decisions we lay out in the following chapters were influenced by two underlying beliefs about what allows effective talent building: differentiation is critical, and development occurs through experiences. These beliefs have implications across a number of processes and provide philosophical direction throughout the many choice points you will encounter in the design process.

Differentiation Is Critical

Easy to espouse but difficult to sustain, differentiation is a foundational element in successful talent management. The heart of talent management is to understand your talent needs and invest appropriately to achieve them. By differentiating your employees based on their current and potential future value to the organization, where to invest becomes clear. If you're unwilling to differentiate—to make the tough calls—then either you are opting to blindly invest while hoping for the right outcome or you are intentionally making investments that will never pay off. Neither choice makes you a good steward of the company's resources.

We believe that differentiation starts with the talent review process we describe in chapter 4. This process gives you complete visibility of the company's leadership—where the talent is deep and high quality, and where it needs more attention. This is a critical step, but it is not differentiation. Differentiation occurs only when you consciously invest greater resources in growing some leaders versus others based on a belief that this will yield a higher future return for the company.

Some people fear differentiation because they feel it will create an in-group and an out-group, or that some segment of the population will be treated unfairly. Quite the contrary, without differentiation, it is literally impossible to treat anyone fairly because "fair" suggests that an appropriate balance exists between an action and a reaction. The companies that manage talent well start with a philosophy that everyone should be highly engaged and have an equal opportunity to have a great career. *After* that baseline is met, the company decides to selectively invest in talent to achieve the best results for the business. Those who are most likely to deliver the most value for the company receive a larger investment. There is nothing unfair about that.

When some people say a system is not fair, they often mean that it is not equal. You will hear this concern expressed as "value the B players" or "we need people who will just show up and work their eight hours." The implication is that those who contribute at a lower level than the very top performers will not be valued. We believe that if these employees are being treated fairly, they will receive the exact amount of value from the company that they have earned. They will not receive what the high potentials receive, but since they will likely not contribute as much in the future, it would be inherently unfair to give them those rewards. (We discuss this further in chapter 4.) Others who argue that differentiation is unfair simply have a world-view that equal treatment is always better than unequal treatment. This may be the vision of utopia for some, but it is anathema to a competitive corporation.

Throughout this book, we provide guidance on how to effectively differentiate your talent and the investment you make in them. You will learn about the performance and potential matrix, simple per-formance management, and the OPTM Competency Matrix, while seeing how the guiding principles of transparency and accountability ensure that differentiation is done correctly.

Development Occurs Through Experiences

It may strike you as counterintuitive that you learn more on a job than you learn in a training course. After all, wasn't the entire point of training programs, executive education, and those years in college to become better at doing your job? The 70-20-10 principle says that most development comes from experiences at work and in life. That is the 70 percent of the 70-20-10 equation. What you learn from others through observing, getting coaching, shadowing, and so on constitutes 20 percent of learning. The time you spend in a classroom makes up about 10 percent of what you learn.[4]

The science behind this belief is not as robust as what we use to support our other points; 70-20-10 is a practitioner and consulting framework, not an academic one. Although there are volumes written on adult learning, we cannot find a body of research that specifically tested 70-20-10. So while the exact percentages are not a proven fact, the idea rests on sound research. And senior HR leaders tend to find this consistent with their observations. "Sending people to classes looks good and feels good, but rarely results in behavior change," says American Express's Kevin Cox. The allocation feels right to us based on our experience, and it heavily guides our approach to development.

Overcoming Objections

At this point, we hope you think that OPTM is a potential solution to your longtime talent-building woes. But you may be a little concerned about the questions and objections that you get from your team, executives, or HR leaders. We have heard a few of these as well, so we would like to equip you in advance with some answers. (In each chapter, we also address the challenges and objections that you will hear about making changes to specific talent practices.)

OPTM does not provide enough information. Managers need more detailed processes and tools to ensure they are carrying out talent management processes correctly.

- Managers need structure, and our approach provides it more effectively than traditional talent management processes by making that structure simple and understandable. Research and practice should guide how much detail they really need; there is no research that says thick instruction manuals are more effective.

- We can include many different design elements in a talent process. However, because simplicity is the key to implementation and only successfully implemented processes can work, the balance between complexity or ease of use and value must always be achieved.

- We need to redefine success in talent management processes as getting results, not as whether managers correctly complete a process endurance course.

- If a process is designed in a simple, value-added way, there should be very little instruction required.

- Not if the cake is easy to make.

OPTM is just a formatting exercise. It sounds like nothing more than reformatting. Coming up with a one page form is not that difficult if we reduce the font size and squeeze the margins on our current form.

- OPTM is not a gimmick. It is both a philosophy and an approach to building talent that focuses on reducing the work required by managers, providing them guidance on tough decisions, and building great talent faster. When doing that well, we are often able to fit that process or information onto one page (or occasionally two).

OPTM will not work. It goes against everything I have ever been taught about how to design HR processes.

- We rely on the same science that you learned; we just found a simpler way to apply it. Even if some of our advice feels new to you, it is all based on well-validated academic research. How about giving it a shot and seeing if it works? If not, you can always go back to what you do today.

- Even if it does not work (but it will), your managers will be impressed that you are trying to make their lives easier.

But we just finished designing that process! I just spent $500,000 on a consulting firm to design the world's greatest performance management system. How will I look if I throw that all away?

- Before you roll out a traditional process with a low chance of success, let's see how our approach can take your great ideas and make them even better. No one will remember that you spent $500,000 if they like the new process and believe that it adds value. They will definitely remember that you spent $500,000 if they do not like it. And you may find elements of the existing system that you can salvage. Design the right process, and if you can identify opportunities to leverage your current infra-structure, by all means do so.

How to Use the Book

The next six chapters explain exactly how to create talent management practices that work. We start by describing how you can make performance management, arguably the least favored corporate process ever, both easy to use and performance enhancing. We then detail how you can develop better talent faster by eliminating complexity and adding value to 360-degree assessments, talent review processes, and engagement surveys, in chapters 3, 4, and 5. Chapter 6 introduces a new process to identify the right competencies for your organization; the concepts in chapter 7 ensure that your talent management practices are sustained over time.

We have structured each chapter in a consistent way, starting with a description of the core science, detailing how to simplify the process while adding value, and suggesting ways to build transparency and accountability into the process. We also address the objections you might hear when proposing a change. This format allows you to start with the topics you are most interested in without having to read the chapters in any particular sequence. We have tried to make each chapter detailed and practical, providing clear guidance for how to design and implement the practice successfully. Each chapter also includes an overview of an OPTM version of the talent practice, complete with sample tools and templates we feel work well. Finally, we provide some questions that allow you to quickly assess how your current practices compare to our OPTM benchmark.

We are confident that, if you take this approach, both you and your executives will be thrilled with the results. Most importantly, if you use OPTM to build better leaders faster, your company will achieve a distinct competitive advantage that your rivals will not soon match.

2

Performance Management

PERHAPS NO TALENT MANAGEMENT process is more important or more reviled than performance management. The presumably simple steps of setting goals, monitoring performance, and evaluating an employee's accomplishments inspire legendary amounts of managerial eye rolling and foot dragging. Yet across the spectrum of HR practices, nothing else is so directly linked to individual and corporate results, making performance management a perfect candidate for OPTM.

The business reasons for performance management are quite simple: align the employee's efforts with business needs and fairly evaluate the employee's performance. Unfortunately, these two simple objectives have become needlessly complex under pressure from managers wanting formulaic systems, lawyers demanding defensible processes, and HR's own attempts to add value. A recent survey showed that only one in ten employees felt that their firm's performance management system actually improved their performance.[1]

The challenge may stem from the fact that performance management's purpose has fundamentally changed over time. Today's systems grew from appraisal systems created in the late 1800s to help eliminate favoritism in the United States Civil Service.[2] Until the late 1950s and 1960s, these systems were used solely to assess performance in a technical, task-focused way. There was no intent to inspire employees to higher performance or to align their actions with the business strategy.

That changed as a groundswell of behavioral research started to emerge in the mid-twentieth century that included Edwin Locke and Gary Latham's groundbreaking work on goal-setting theory and Victor Vroom's foundational concept of expectancy theory.[3] These theories provided the impetus and scientific justification for taking a more comprehensive approach to managing performance. Our brief descriptions do not adequately honor the landmark nature of this research, but they highlight the core science you should rely on to create your one page performance management process.

Step 1. Start with the Science

The incredibly rich research on motivating performance makes designing a performance management process easier than you might have thought. The four studies we summarize next highlight the most consequential findings for the design process.

The Harder the Goal, the More It Motivates

That stretch goals really do motivate higher performance than non-stretch goals is no myth. There is a linear relationship between a goal's difficulty and the amount of effort and performance the goal produces. That relationship is true no matter how challenging the goal is, which means a moderately challenging goal will motivate higher performance than an easy goal, and a hard goal will motivate more than a moderately challenging one. The only time motivation drops is if you physically just cannot work any harder toward the goal or it becomes so difficult that you stop being committed to it.[4]

Goals Aligned with Self-Interest Motivate the Most

Self-interest is a powerful motivational tool. The more likely we are to feel good when a goal is accomplished, the more motivational that goal will be. A goal causes us to be motivated if: (1) we anticipate we will be happy if the goal is accomplished, (2) we feel our performance is linked to rewards, and (3) our effort will actually result in the goal being accomplished.[5] While not every goal can always meet these three standards, managers should not expect great performance unless employees' goals reflect "what is in it for them."

Specific Goals Create Higher Performance Than Urging, "Do Your Best"

Underlying the entire concept of goal setting is the expectation that an employee with specific goals will perform better on a task than someone with less clear goals. Experiments show that urging employees to "do your best" on a task never resulted in as high a performance as when specific performance goals were set.[6] Managers should be careful about setting goals too narrowly, however, since that can cause a phenomenon called inattentional blindness.[7] In that state, employees are so focused on one outcome that they ignore important information that could increase their performance, improve their learning, or ensure their ethical behavior.[8]

Too Many Goals Reduce the Effort on Each One

An emerging body of research indicates that the more goals an individual has, the more poorly he performs on each. There is no insight yet as to the ideal number of goals, but this does suggest that every goal added after a limited number is detrimental to that individual's overall performance.[9] Researchers found that reduced performance was most likely when another goal was added to an existing set, such as when high-potential employees receive another "special project."[10]

The science provides clear direction on how to make a performance management process successful. Build a system that gets people committed to a few, challenging goals and give them feedback along the way. Although very little research exists on how to actually construct such a system, our approach can help guide the way.

Step 2. Eliminate Complexity, Add Value

Although most managers understand the benefit of setting clear goals and evaluating performance, typically complex performance management processes can quickly sap their motivation. Our approach faithfully applies the science to create a simple, easy-to-use process that managers are sure to love. You might be surprised how little it takes to make this process work.

Use a Simple Form

Managers around the world annually suffer through four, seven, or even ten-page performance management forms. The form is just a mechanism for recording how to achieve that core business objective, ensuring that employees understand their goals and that they are fairly evaluated at year-end. This requires only three items for each goal on the list: a simple description of the goal (see SIMple, next), a metric for determining if the goal is achieved, and a space for recording the results. That's it. Later in this chapter, we elaborate on why the bells and whistles on typical performance forms are not needed.

Keep Goals SIMple, Not SMART

You may be familiar with the acronym SMART (specific, measurable, achievable, realistic, and time-bound) to describe a well-written goal. That is a great acronym, but it is possible to go one (or two) better. Most managers are not likely to be setting unachievable and unrealistic goals, so we can delete these two SMART adjectives with little risk that goal quality will suffer. Also, if a goal is specific, that should incorporate the concept of time—for example, get *x* done by *y*—so we can drop time-bound as a separate consideration.

What SMART leaves out are two important factors—the relevance of the goal to the organization and the relevance of the goal to the individual. One is critical for the company to achieve its results, and the other is critical to motivate the employee to higher performance (remember self-interest). If we add the concept of *importance* to what makes a great goal, we end up with specific, important, measurable—SIMple goal setting. Goals structured this way will meet the key criteria for motivational goals; they are specific and challenging. Making them measurable is as simple as either including a metric in the goal (e.g., increase sales by 20 percent) or listing a metric separately (e.g., customer satisfaction increases by 10 percent). Some additional guidelines will help you keep goals SIMple.

Focus on the Vital Few. We know that having too many goals leads to reduced effort on each one, but getting to the right number is more art than science. We believe the right number is something more than one and something less than five—we suggest three. Here is our logic: if the goals are really important—big, challenging, having impact—it seems unlikely that someone can achieve more than three or four over the course of a year.

The research supports this approach, finding that too many goals can reduce overall performance in two ways. First, if a person has to achieve different outcomes on a single goal (e.g., increase quality and quantity of production), the result will likely be lower performance on each metric than what he could have achieved if he had tried to maximize performance on one goal. Second, when someone has multiple separate goals, if she is asked to increase the performance on one, the performance on the others will decrease.

In addition, by the time a person gets to four goals, at least one of them becomes much less meaningful from a rewards perspective. At five goals, one is now likely worth less than 20 percent of a bonus or rating—is this still meaningful? Not everything that a manager or employee does needs to be listed on the goal form. We all have parts of our job that do not rise to the level of an important goal. We suggest you allow a maximum of four goals on your OPTM performance management tool.

Do Not Specify Certain Goals as "Stretch" Goals. The science is clear that bigger goals generate more effort, but there is no science suggesting that having "stretch" goals is better than just designing every goal with the right balance of stretch and achievability. If you define a goal as stretch, you are either saying that the other goals are not that challenging or this goal is nearly impossible to achieve. We prefer putting the right degree of stretch into every goal and dropping the separate label. It is needless complexity.

Do Not Include Goal Weighting. This goal is worth 20 percent of a bonus or rating, that one is 25 percent, the other is 35 percent. The typical intent of weighting is to show the employee which goals are more important than others and to provide a precise method to determine rewards. In reality, goal weighting removes managerial discretion and creates a false sense of precision. (Is that goal *really* worth 8 percent more than the other? Is a 2.6 out of 5 really worse than a 2.7?) There is a simpler way. List the goals in order of importance on the performance management form and tell the employee that all goals are important, but that the ones listed first matter the most.

Set Employees' Goals

Allowing employees to participate in setting their goals does not seem like a particularly horrible concept. After all, they are closest to the work, so shouldn't they know exactly what they can achieve? Plus, it would make sense that they would work harder to achieve goals they set themselves as opposed to goals imposed by a manager. In fact, if your view of the workplace is more socialistic than capitalistic, you might even argue that employees must be involved in setting their goals.

Unfortunately, our intuition fails us on this one. The research on participative goal setting found that there is no difference in performance whether an employee or a manager sets a goal. The studies found that higher performance is a function of various other factors, but is independent of who actually set the goal.

Much of the support for participatory goal setting is based on research that seems to indicate that this positively affects performance by increasing an employee's commitment to the goal.[11] However, subsequent research has shown that there are other, equally effective methods for gaining that commitment, such as a manager's explanation of the rationale or importance of each goal. Therefore, utilizing participative goal setting in the performance management process adds complexity without providing any measurable benefit.[12]

Give Frequent Feedback on Progress

The research is clear that if people are committed to a goal, they will redirect (or redouble) efforts if they learn that they are not headed for success. Thus, feedback becomes a surefire way to increase the performance of any employee against any well-set goal. We understand that many managers harbor an irrational fear of giving feedback. We can relieve much of that fear through a process called "feed-forward" and the daily questions process we describe in chapter 3.

Frequent feedback builds leaders faster because each time people receive feedback or feed-forward, they have an opportunity to correct their course. More frequent feedback shortens the performance improvement cycle, and actual improvement occurs faster. How often a manager should give feedback depends on employees' goals, their competence, and their performance; the manager has a great opportunity to be transparent with each employee about when he or she will get feedback and why.

Solicit Formal or Informal 360-Degree Feedback on Performance

As with the talent review process, a calibration of opinions is a sure way to get an accurate rating. For any goal that is not directly measurable and whose performance involves someone other than the direct manager, get input from everyone who can realistically observe if and how the employee achieved that goal. Many employees and most managers have ten or more stakeholders or clients whom they serve, and the average of their opinions is likely the closest to the objective truth.

Each of these elements adds more value for managers and employees than it adds complexity to the overall process. If you use only these guidelines to create the performance management process, we're confident that your managers will love it.

There are also several elements that, while possibly veering into questionable territory on the Complexity-Value Curve, might be appropriate depending on the organization's holistic process approach and culture. At a minimum, they do not contradict the science and are not inherently wrong to build into the process. So if appropriate, you can consider the following elements.

Evaluate Behaviors as Part of Performance Management. This might seem like an easy element to add. Many of us believe that by measuring behaviors, we can balance how things get done with what gets done. Without these elements included in the performance management process, the fear is that managers will do anything necessary to get results, leaving a trail of destruction behind them. Although HR professionals or business leaders would agree that proper behaviors are critical to a manager's success, you can reinforce the importance of those behaviors in many ways. You can use a development plan (that is, one with teeth) to hold managers accountable for changing their behaviors. You can use a talent review or succession planning process to send a clear message that good managerial behaviors will get you ahead and poor ones will hold you back. You can use the results of a 360-degree assessment as a metric to reinforce what to change. You can even use a very strong corporate culture to send messages about which behaviors are acceptable.

Before you make a choice to include behaviors in the performance management plan, consider all the other ways that you can influence how managers behave. Is this really the best place to hold them accountable for their behaviors?

If you do choose to include behaviors, you need to decide whether to include them at the same level as performance goals (e.g., a manager is required to achieve specific behavioral improvement goals), as an overall category (did the manager demonstrate the required behaviors in general?), or as reminders (include one or two behaviors that are important to focus on this year). We have seen variations of each work effectively. You need to decide where the value-complexity trade-off lies in each approach for your organization. Also, like performance goals, behavioral goals should be specific, important, and measurable.

There are a few other considerations in evaluating behaviors:

The size and complexity of the behavior, capability, or competency model. Are you going to ask managers to be rated against eight competencies with fifteen behavioral statements under each? You are probably way over the limit if you want to reduce complexity. (See our thoughts in chapter 6 on competencies.)

Measuring behaviors. Is there an objective measurement tool? A 360-degree or other multi-rater feedback is a fair way to evaluate behaviors or progress against them.

Rewarding behaviors. Will performance be a threshold for a rating or reward (some minimum behavioral standard must be met) or will it be a cap (no rating or reward higher than X unless behavioral standards are met)? Or will behaviors have no impact at all, which would suggest they should not be included?

Overall, we support including behaviors in a performance management process. As you can see from all the choices, however, complexity can slip into this process all too easily. Most managers do not mind being held responsible for good behaviors. The best managers *love* being held responsible for them (easy points at performance review time!). What you want to avoid is a heavy-handed, multipage process that seems far removed from the simple goal of having managers behave properly.

Mike Markovits, vice president of business and technical leadership at IBM, suggests a simple approach for wiring behaviors to performance: "If you score below average as a people manager, you cannot receive the top performance rating." For organizations that have mechanisms to measure manager quality, a similar straightforward link may work well. For others, accountability on behaviors may be more effective if embedded into the talent review or other processes.

Force a Distribution or Ranking. The words, "forced ranking" are sure to agitate most managers and set off fierce debates among HR leaders. Popularized by General Electric and given notoriety when Ford Motor Co. was sued for its process, a forced distribution or ranking is a legitimate addition to the performance management process, with solid science to back it. Forced ranking, if actions are taken against the results, will inarguably improve the performance of the business.

In a study to simulate how performance would be affected if a company removed the bottom 10 percent of performers each year over thirty years, researchers concluded that "results suggest that a forced ranking system could lead to noticeable improvement in workforce potential, that most of the improvement should be expected to occur over the first several years, and that improvement is largely a function of the percentage of workers to be fired and the level of voluntary turnover." They added that "results showed that a forced ranking system can improve workforce potential, in the sense that, on average, lower-potential workers can be identified and replaced by workers with higher potential."[13]

Given that the benefits of such a program often emerge in the first few years, some organizations may find it appropriate to adjust the forced distribution over time. For example, a company that has terminated poor performers effectively for several years may lower the guidance on the poor-performer segment of the distribution, or different businesses may receive different guidance based on business results. The key here is to ensure there is some guidance on the distribution of the performance rating that is both monitored and enforced. Without clear parameters and follow-up action, ratings inflation will run rampant and erode the effectiveness of the entire performance management process.

Integrate Development Plans with Performance Plans. The research shows no conclusive benefit to either separating or combining performance and development discussions. Some research indicates that discussing pay and advancement during performance feedback makes employees more satisfied with the process, but it does not affect performance. Many HR and business leaders are passionate on this topic one way or another. Our advice is to do what works for your organization.

Some of the most ubiquitous components of performance management programs simply do not have the science or fact-based support to justify all the effort they require. In addition, they can be downright confusing and risk sending misleading messages to employees. We have listed some elements next that we strongly recommend that you do not incorporate.

Do Not Use Labels or Numerical Ratings. A performance management rating scale does not have to include a numerical rating, and we prefer that it does not, at least not one that is communicated to employees. Numerical coding is effective for storing ratings in a performance management system, but telling a person that he is a "three" on a five-point scale does not really compare to telling him that he "met all goals." In fact, managers who want to avoid communicating the actual performance level often use numbers as crutches.

Equally obfuscating are ratings labels, such as star performer, highly valued, or valued contributor. As a consequence of not wanting anyone to feel bad, managers have created proxies for what they really mean—"you exceeded your goals," "you met your goals," or "you did not meet your goals." But since transparency is more effective than euphemisms, rating labels get in the way of effective performance communication.

In our quest for simplicity in design, numbers or labels also become an additional element of complexity that adds no value. They were originally intended to represent something else—how effectively or completely the employee achieved his or her goals. Instead of numbers or labels, say what you mean, for example, "goals were met," or "goals were exceeded."

Do Not Obsess Over the Rating Scale. No subject causes more buzz when HR professionals get together than which performance management scale their company uses. Whether they use three, four, or five choices (or more!), the discussion elicits passionate discussion of why one works better than another. The three-point scale, you will be told, allows you to differentiate the top performers and bottom performers, and that is all that really matters. Four-point advocates tell you it forces participants to choose whether an employee is above or below average. Five-point fans say it fits with the normal curve of performance (which in itself is a fallacy—employee performance doesn't follow a bell-curved distribution). As passionate as you may be about your personal favorite, there is clear evidence that:

> *The number of points does not matter.* Anything between three and seven points has similar levels of scale and rater reliability.[14]

> *The format of the scale does not matter.* There is no evidence that behaviorally anchored scales (those with definitions for what each point means) are more effective than straight numerical scales.[15]

> *Managers tend to use only the higher ratings.* Unless you are forcing a distribution, managers will consistently avoid using the bottom of the scale.[16]

Do Not Include Self-Assessments. Managers commonly ask their employees to conduct a self-assessment at performance review time. This might be done to save the manager from having to write the review herself, because she is genuinely interested in how employees think they have performed or because she believes that there is a benefit in having the employee participate in the process. While each could be beneficial in some way, they both add complexity and ignore the fact that self-assessments are the least accurate form of assessment.[17]

In addition, the research is clear that the less competent someone is, the more delusional he or she is likely to be about his or her performance. So while the ninetieth percentile performer may think he is a ninetieth percentile performer, so do the sixtieth, fortieth, and twentieth percentile performers. A written self-appraisal does nothing more than damage most employees' pride when their self-review does not align with the manager's view.

Another reason not to ask for self-assessments is that an employee's view of his or her performance really should not matter. This may sound unduly harsh, but the performance review is a time for the manager to tell the employee his or her perceptions of their performance. There can be dialogue, but not negotiation. Why ask for the employee's opinion when, at the end of the day, it is not going to matter in the final evaluation? Self-assessments are needless complexity wrapped in the mantle of "everyone's opinion matters."

Step 3. Create Transparency and Accountability

A great way to build trust within your organization is to ensure that the performance process is transparent and that leaders are held accountable for execution. Both objectives become much easier with a simple process such as the one we have just described.

Transparency

A key benefit of transparency in performance management is that employees will feel that they have been fairly evaluated. Remember that a key driver of commitment to goals is the belief that achieving them will lead to rewards. There are two areas in performance management where transparency is most relevant—the goal-setting or evaluation process and the distribution of ratings (if one exists).

Share Goal Sources and Linkages. Employees should understand where goals originate and how they will be evaluated. Do goals flow from a larger set of corporate or departmental objectives? What impact does their achievement have on department or company results? Managers can share this information via a conversation during the process or through material posted on the intranet. Employees should also understand who has input into their evaluation.

Share Rating Scales and Distribution. If you have a target distribution or forced ranking of performance ratings, share it. Even more powerful, share the actual distribution results if they are not forced. When employees know that 12 percent of the people in their department exceeded all of their goals and 34 percent exceeded some of them, they will have a better benchmark of their own performance.

Accountability

If you are a manager, you have probably had to be prodded on occasion to complete your performance reviews. If you are in HR, you have likely struggled at some point to get managers to complete this seemingly straightforward task. Accountability is a key driver of performance management success. If an organization is not setting goals, coaching, and doing fair evaluations, it is not leveraging a huge driver of performance. There are a few different ways to approach accountability in this area, some more heavy-handed than others. Here are a few suggestions:

- *Withholding a manager's bonus until he completes every review.* Threat-based but very effective, this method likely will have to be used only once.

- *Withholding the staff's bonuses until the manager completes every review.* Withholding the staff's bonuses until the manager does the reviews and letting the staff know why they are not being paid is the most draconian method to drive accountability. (If the manager is this bad, it is probably just as easy to fire her.)

- *Employee-driven accountability.* Tell the employees a month in advance exactly how the process should work and the timing. Let them know that if their manager does not fulfill his responsibilities to set goals and check in or conduct the final review, the employees should remind the manager. If he still does not complete the process, they should remind HR. We call this "time-bomb communication" because you have set a time bomb and given the manager exact instructions how to defuse it (simply have the conversation). If he chooses not to defuse it, it is going to blow up.

- *CEO-driven accountability.* A CEO, who is a role model for this behavior, can be a powerful driver. When the highest-powered executive in the company shows that she can find the time to do performance reviews, other people's excuses for not participating look rather weak.

In Summary: The OPTM Performance Management Process

Our performance management approach can radically improve clarity and increase commitment to goals, while reducing the time spent on the process. Although the overall process steps (set goals, check in on progress, evaluate goals) may not differ from the process you currently use, little else remains the same. Our sample performance management form focuses on only the most important elements—the goal and its metric (see figure 2-1). We increase focus by limiting the number of goals to four. We do not worry about how many points are on the rating scale, individually weighting goals, cute labels for each rating category, or any of the bells and whistles that complicate traditional approaches to performance management.

FIGURE 2-1

OPTM Performance Management Template

	Name:		Date of review:	
Performance	Goal #1		Metric:	
	Results:			
	Goal #2		Metric:	
	Results:			
	Goal #3		Metric:	
	Results:			
	Goal #4		Metric:	
	Results:			
Behaviors	Goal #1		Metric:	
	Results:			
	Goal #2		Metric:	
	Results:			
	Overall results:	Met expectations		

Overcoming Objections

I have a very technical group of clients who like precision. They insist on having goal weightings and a precise numerical rating in the performance management system.

Your clients take comfort in precision because they are used to consistent measurement standards—an inch is always an inch and a kilogram is always a kilogram. The same is not true in performance management because there is no objective standard against which to measure performance. A 2.6 rating on a 5-point scale could actually be anywhere between a 1.6 and a 3.6, depending on who is doing the rating. "Assessing performance involves judgment; it is relative and can't just rely on a formula," says Lucien Alziari, senior vice president of HR at Avon Products. "If you think [a formula] is giving employees certainty, you are fooling both them and yourself." Once managers understand these realities, it becomes obvious that what appears to be precision is in reality just sloppy measurement.

I have a system that you might say is complex, but it seems to work well for my company. Why should I change?

It is great that your current system works. Do you think your line managers would like your current system better if it took half as long to complete goal setting and performance review?

We have HR technology that dictates how our performance management process works. It will be very difficult, not to mention expensive, to change this.

There is no easy answer for that. Technology should never dictate any talent process. However, if you are stuck with the technology, see how many of the bells and whistles can be turned off to simplify the process. That is typically a low-cost intervention. If the process is not completely static, see if you can customize it to better meet the OPTM philosophy. Moving into slightly more expensive territory, some human resource information systems (HRIS) technology allows you to buy and integrate a different front end on the system. This front end can be highly customized to make your client's experience faster and easier. Finally, give your HRIS leader a copy of this book.

Assess Your Performance Management Process

- Is enough information about corporate, functional, or regional objectives available to help you determine your goals?

- Do at least 85 percent of employees have a high-quality conversation about their performance with their manager at least twice a year?

- What does your employee survey say about how effective your performance management process is?

- Does it take the average manager more than twenty minutes to complete the form? Is there a limit to the number of goals (ideally less than five)?

3

360-Degree Feedback

THE INCREASING POPULARITY OF 360-degree assessments (360s) seems to rely on a rock-solid stream of logic. Leaders' behaviors are important to the organization because well-behaved leaders balance what gets done with how things get done. This balance increases their own effectiveness and their team's engagement and performance, which translates into superior financial results. So if we regularly give leaders 360-degree feedback, they will be motivated to improve their behaviors and the average quality of leaders and results will continually increase. It is a wonderful theory, but it bears little resemblance to reality.

Although 360s can help build better talent faster and therefore improve an organization's results, few see these benefits, and for obvious reasons. The typical 360-degree process relies on a self-motivated manager who readily accepts the 360 feedback, commits to self-improvement, and moves forward with an action plan. Most firms do not require any action planning after the assessment, and only 20 percent even require that participants speak to their managers about the results. Also, typical 360-degree reports are difficult to understand, do not focus managers on the right actions, and do not provide practical advice about what to do next. Why so few leaders improve purely as a result of receiving 360-degree feedback is not hard to understand.

Despite these challenges, we strongly support the 360-degree assessment process because we believe that it is a simple and powerful way to achieve the business objective of aligning people's behaviors with the organization's needs. "There is no better way to identify truly gifted leaders, versus those who 'manage up' well," says Kevin Cox at American Express.

In this chapter, we focus exclusively on 360s that measure or provide direction on behaviors. Those used to evaluate performance are helpful as well; we addressed those briefly in chapter 2. To understand how 360-degree feedback can improve organizational performance, let's start with what the science does and does not say about the process.

Step 1. Start with the Science

As 360s first gained popularity in the late 1980s and early 1990s, there were few academic studies that reviewed their effectiveness.[1] Even today, most of the available research is related to various individual components of a 360—whether feedback increases performance, who the raters should be, how different scales work, and so on. Unfortunately, this leaves ample ground for practitioners and consultants to design and implement 360-degree programs without the guidance of clear facts. Here's what the science says:

Feedback Can Improve Performance

At the heart of any feedback process is the assumption that feedback leads to behavior changes that improve the performance of a task. The 360-degree process has little value unless this assumption is true.

The problem is that this assumption was built on questionable science, and practitioners are only now beginning to understand how feedback affects performance.

The assumption emerged from research in the mid-twentieth century despite evidence within the exact same studies that directly contradicted those claims. In a seminal article in 1956, Robert Ammons reviewed and summarized previous studies on the link between feedback and performance, concluding that "knowledge of performance" (feedback) increases motivation and learning.[2] The article became the standard reference to cite when conducting other experiments about, and justifying the use of, feedback. Surprisingly, many of Ammons's conclusions relied on data that he admitted "[had] been collected informally" or "inferred" from other experiments— not quite the hard proof desired to justify one of the most popular HR tools.

Our understanding of the feedback-performance relationship increased thanks to a 1996 meta-analysis of 607 different studies that examined the feedback-to-performance link.[3] That study concluded that feedback generally did improve performance (on average by 0.4 standard deviations), but it also found that performance actually decreased more than one-third of the time that feedback was given. This research showed that the level of improvement decreased as the feedback became less about a task and more about the individual as a person.[4] In short, the study found that if you tell someone how to more effectively produce a widget based on his past performance, he will probably do it better. However, if you tell him that he needs to talk less in team meetings, it is much less likely that feedback alone will change his behavior.

The most conclusive statement we can make is that feedback alone *can* change behavior, but it is certainly not guaranteed. This means that conducting 360s without structured follow-up is likely to be a poor use of an organization's resources. Some would say that, even without any organizational benefit, 360-degree feedback is a worthy investment because it increases personal awareness. We reject that view. If the objective is greater personal awareness that does not improve performance, that activity should take place outside the boundaries of the organization.

Clear Goals for Improvement Help Behavior Change

The research indicates that one of the few things that drive behavior change is having clear goals for improvement. The limited research shows that having goals increases the likelihood, but by no means guarantees, that someone who receives feedback will take action on it.[5] The goal-setting theories discussed in chapter 2 provide additional weight to the proposition that feedback and goals are the most effective combination.

Personality Influences One's Response to Feedback

That personalities play a role in how people receive and respond to feedback is not surprising. Individuals' personality traits influence emotions, sense of self-esteem, and thought processes, so they are going to see feedback through those lenses. For example, the more easily someone tolerates the typical ups and downs in life (personality theory calls this emotional stability), the more motivated he is to take action on feedback.[6] If a person is an extrovert, she is more likely to ask for additional feedback. If she is more self-disciplined and thorough (personality theory calls this conscientiousness), she is more likely to participate in developmental activities.[7] Because different people have different levels of these personality traits, managers will react to feedback in varying ways.

Following Up on Feedback Positively Increases Perceptions of Change

In a study of more than ten thousand managers across a number of companies, Marshall Goldsmith confirmed what may seem intuitive—if you follow up on your feedback, people will say you have improved.[8] And, the more they think you have followed up, the greater improvement they will say you have made. This one simple link to results—follow-up—had been missing from the academic literature but provides powerful guidance in creating an OPTM process.

Step 2. Eliminate Complexity, Add Value

Based on the science we have covered, we have some facts that can inform what is required for an effective 360-degree process. We know that feedback can help motivate change, but it is possible for people to change without explicit feedback. We know that having goals can prompt someone to take action, but it is far from guaranteed. We know that everyone responds differently to feedback, but that nearly everyone who follows up on feedback is perceived as trying to change.

So we start the 360-degree design process guided by the limited science and applying what we call the "watercooler maxim": everyone at work knows how a person behaves, and the organization is already responding to it; the 360 just captures that knowledge on paper. We mention the watercooler maxim because many authors imply that the information from 360s is somehow independent of other social systems in the organization. They urge that 360s should be confidential, purely for development, and have no consequences for inaction on the results. For these authors, no one gossips, no one talks about someone's behaviors around the watercooler, and no one has already judged her because of them. It is almost as if some people believe that keeping a 360 confidential will prevent anyone from knowing how someone behaves. If you have worked in any organization from GE to the Girl Scouts, you know that is a ridiculously naive assumption. Unfortunately, it drives a level of secrecy and near-piety among some consultants about how and when to use 360-degree assessment results.

Our starting proposition is that 360-degree behavioral feedback presents critical information about a manager's performance—how closely his or her behaviors meet the organization's needs. We are not sure why a company should withhold this information from people who could help improve the behaviors or from those who need it to make decisions on allocating an organization's resources (e.g., promotions, recognition). After all, as the watercooler maxim says, it is not a secret—the 360 just provides a consistent way to gather and present that data.

Our second proposition is that we should make it as easy as possible for managers to take action on the survey feedback. Consistent with our OPTM philosophy, implementation is paramount and anything that eases it should be done. To keep the survey report actionable, we set a high standard—that the person receiving a 360 report should know *what to do* by the time he or she reads the first two pages. Sound impossible? We have built a 360-degree assessment that meets this standard and tested it on more than three hundred participants. It relies on the core science and is guided by the principles of feed-forward—that people are most receptive to advice for change when it is focused on future (not past) behaviors and provides specific examples of how to change.[9]

The 360 process can be divided in two parts: completing the survey and following up on the results. If you plan on building your own 360, the following advice will guide you through the design process.

If you plan on purchasing an assessment process from a vendor, find one that fits as closely as possible the design that we describe.

Eliminating Complexity

The typical 360 presents a great opportunity to eliminate complexity and make managers more productive. Achieving simplicity might be easier than you think. Kevin Wilde, chief learning officer of General Mills, recently told us that by adopting an OPTM mind-set, General Mills reduced its 360 report from fifty pages to eight. By following our procedures, you can make similar progress.

Use a Practical Scale. A good 360-degree scale should preserve the participant's ego and make it easy for him or her to understand the results and take action. Most scales fail on both counts.

- *Preserve egos.* An intuitive finding from the research is that feedback that hurts self-esteem is going to be less motivational. Most 360s start with a strong disadvantage because the scale is almost guaranteed to hit the self-esteem of at least half the people who use it. The scales are typically numerical, from one to five, with labels to describe each point (i.e., strongly agree to strongly disagree). The groups that give feedback are charted on that scale. There are details that include average scores within the company, benchmark scores, change from previous scores, and so on.

  If a person's positive view of himself is validated by the results, he is likely to be happy and unmotivated to change. If he feels that the results portray him in a way that is inconsistent with his self-image, he is likely to resist the feedback by denying its validity. He might claim that the responding participants were not representative, that the feedback reflects behaviors that he *had* to show because of a unique business challenge, or the data is simply wrong—he does not behave like that. Either way, a scale that displays results so that a score below neutral leaves participants feeling as though they have failed some objective benchmark is likely to leave many unmotivated to act on the results.

- *Make action easy.* The complexity and detail in a typical 360 report make it difficult for any manager to understand what conclusions to draw and how to develop an action plan. The typical 360 requires the average manager to sit with an HR leader to interpret the report and then wander through a thick book of suggestions or a Web site to create an action plan. Wouldn't this process be easier if survey raters were just asked to articulate what the individual should do differently and how, and that information was then shared with the participant?

If the goal of 360 feedback is to change a manager's behavior, a much better approach is to tell her what behaviors she needs to do more and which to do less. This allows a participant to understand what should change, in which direction, and to what extreme. The scale we recommend provides exactly that information. The components of our OPTM 360-degree scale are "do much more, do more, don't change, do less, do much less." When a person gets feedback on this scale, taking action instantly becomes easier. We show how in the next section, and we make it even better when we add value later in this chapter.

Ask the Fewest Possible Questions. If we apply the core principle of "the least amount of information necessary to make the best decision," it should raise questions about why seventy, ninety, or even a hundred twenty items appear on many 360s. Long questionnaires make the process difficult for raters and may reduce their willingness to participate in the future. Long questionnaires also mean long reports, with more information that the manager needs to sort through and interpret. Providing managers with clear information about how to change their behaviors using fewer questions is quite possible. The following items explain how to avoid excessive length:

- *Identify the most critical behaviors to change.* Most 360-degree items are derived from either a company's leadership competency model or an external best-practice model that purports to identify the characteristics of an ideal leader. Two things typically go wrong in this process. First, the survey items tend to include every behavior in the competency model, rather than a narrower set of the most important behaviors. While many of the behaviors may be part of what makes a leader successful, some are more important than others. Asking the 360-degree participants to respond to noncritical questions makes the assessment fail the value-complexity test. To ensure success, ask only the fifteen or twenty-five most important items. Second, your company might use certain idioms or colloquial phrases (e.g., "Walk the talk" or "bureaucracy buster") that would mean more to the participants than an item found in a generic 360.

- *Ask direct questions on behavior, not concepts.* When a 360 is designed to measure someone's level of competence in a particular area, there are certain academic rules to follow for a valid result. Construct validity, internal validity, and other concerns mean that you must ask three, four, five, or more items to prove that you are accurately measuring a particular construct (e.g., being results oriented). The survey gets longer, and interpretation of the results becomes more complex.

You can keep the 360 lean by including simply worded items about specific behaviors (e.g., "Gives me frequent feedback on my performance") and combining them with the "do more—do less" scale. There is no need to prove construct validity when including items in this way.

A manager who sees the responses to that item understands which behaviors matter and knows if she should behave in this way more or less often. The overall result is a shorter, easily understood report that managers are more likely to use.

Present Results with Simple, Clean Graphics. There is a lot going through a manager's head when she gets her 360 report back. If you overwhelm her with the amount of data or confuse her with the way it's presented, the report becomes an impediment to action. In a quick Web search, we found assessment results that were presented in a spider diagram, a triangle, five different types of charts on the same page, and other significant violations of the "least amount of information needed" rule. You should seek the simplest possible way to present this information so the manager easily understands it. In most cases, that is going to be a basic bar chart or marks on a continuum.

Report Only Value-Adding Data. A few features typically used in 360 reports do not do much to enhance understanding and can be misleading. Eliminating them results in both a cleaner, more effective report.

- *Do not include normative data ("norms").* Research suggests that feedback comparing people to an external standard is less motivational than providing specific advice for change. Knowing that someone is at the twentieth or eightieth percentile does less than just telling him what he needs to do differently.

- *Do not report on strengths.* You might have noticed that we have not discussed strengths anywhere. Reinforcing a leader's strengths in a 360 is not wrong, but since the purpose of the 360 is to guide behavior change, the focus should remain on key behavioral action items. If you feel it is useful to include strengths, ensure that the placement and space dedicated to them is secondary to the action items.

- *Do not report high scores and low scores.* In many 360 reports, these scores are both meaningless and misleading. Are they the most important? Should someone change those behaviors a little or a lot? The "Add Value" steps later in this chapter show which items are priorities.

The PepsiCo Manager Quality Performance Index

PepsiCo is serious about giving its managers feedback and holding them accountable for leadership behaviors. It is also seriously efficient in how it does that. The company has two powerful feedback tools at its disposal—an organizational health survey and a comprehensive 360. It has also developed a twelve-question Manager Quality Performance Index (MQPI) as a quick, easy way to measure manager quality. The MQPI is a model of OPTM. It focuses on a few, critical behaviors that PepsiCo leaders need to display, such as getting their team to act on the right priorities and effectively working with people different from themselves. The process is transparent; all participants know what the tool is and what it is used for, thanks to communication from senior leadership. And it is an annual process with clear accountability—managers use the data as input into year-end people ratings.

Use the 360 for Both Evaluation and Development. As long as the 360 is one data point among many, this data can be considered when evaluating a leader. It should never be used independently. Talent reviews, succession planning, and assignment or project selections are all valid times to use this information if it is available. There should always be complete transparency about which organizational decisions it can affect. If the 360 is purely for self-awareness—a laudable goal but not related to improved individual performance—it is best done on one's own time.

Keep Responses Anonymous. One of the few commonly accepted practices that we agree with, giving feedback anonymously ensures accuracy and encourages participation. If any portion of a respondent's responses are identifiable (e.g., verbatim quotes), clearly and repeatedly state that in the survey material.

Avoid Self-Assessments. Not including a self-assessment in a 360 may seem odd since nearly all popular 360 tools do. Knowing the gaps between how a person is seen (and likely acts) and how others see him seems like essential information to help him understand what should change and why. However, current research casts serious doubt on the value of self-assessment. One reason given for self-assessments is that people are wired to try to close the gaps between others' views of themselves and their self-view (control theory).

In theory, if people see a gap between their self-rating and how others perceive them, it causes such a level of internal discomfort that they are motivated to close that gap and their behavior changes. Whether this actually works in practice is widely debated. Other research indicates that people are just as likely to explain away the gap with excuses about the rater's credibility or why they needed to act that way due to the demands of the organization. While these are theoretical arguments, additional facts should discourage self-assessment:

- *Self-assessments are inaccurate.* People tend to be consistently inaccurate when rating themselves. Research shows that self-ratings do not correlate with anyone else's ratings—peers, supervisors, direct reports, clients—whether measuring skills, leadership behaviors, performance, or personality traits.[10]

- *They can reduce motivation to change.* Feedback that harms self-esteem makes motivation to change less likely. A large gap between people's self-ratings and others' ratings can create embarrassment that is completely counterproductive to achieving their goals.

- *Self-assessments can misdirect actions.* People may focus on the largest gaps between themselves and others, when these are not the most critical issues to address. As a consequence, a manager may spend significant effort changing behaviors that may not matter.

- *They focus on today's problems, not tomorrow's solutions.* The feedforward philosophy we have discussed says that focusing on how to change in the future is much more productive than evaluating the past or present. Self-ratings focus squarely on today's gaps, for example, "look at these gaps—I'm really embarrassed by them." Without self ratings, the report simply says, "here's what to do going forward."

Adding Value

Whenever we help a manager understand complex information it is a great opportunity to apply the OPTM principle of adding value. The data from a 360-degree assessment likely contains at least a hundred twenty separate data points (if done succinctly with four categories of respondents and thirty items), which take a while to understand and can easily overwhelm a manager. We can add value by distilling this data into information that the manager can quickly understand and apply. Next we explain how we combine our do more—do less scale with a process to prioritize items to create the OPTM 360.

Prioritize the Key Action Items. The OPTM 360 is brief, but the participant still receives data from thirty different items. We know that some of these items are likely more important than others, so we've structured the survey so that respondents prioritize the items (see figure 3-1):

- *Screen 1.* The first survey screen asks respondents to choose their answers using the do more—do less scale. They select answers to each question and then click the "next" button.

- *Screen 2.* After submitting those answers, a second screen lists every item that the respondents marked as do much more, do more, do less or do much less—those items where they indicated something should change. They then select the three items that are the highest priorities for the individual to change. They can select up to three, but no more than three, items. They then click the "next" button.

- *Screen 3.* On the following screen, the three items selected are listed. The respondents are asked to write a suggestion for what the participant should stop, start, or continue doing to improve the behavior. They have now completed the entire survey in ten minutes or less.

FIGURE 3-1

Example of OPTM 360 Assessment

What this is: The One Page Talent Management 360 provides the participant with focused and specific advice about which behaviors to develop and how.

How it works: You will tell the participant which behaviors you believe are their priorities for change. You will also be asked to provide a suggestion for what they should start, stop, or continue doing to improve each of those behaviors. How you rate the participant is anonymous, but your comments will be shown as written *if* your priority questions are among the top three selected by all raters.

What you do: Complete the questions on each of the three screens openly and honestly. Remember that if your comments appear on the survey report, they will be exactly as you have written them. Taking this survey should take ten minutes or less.

If you have any questions before you begin, please contact your local human resources leader.

In the following areas, how should this person change his or her behavior or actions?	Do much less	Do less	Do not change	Do more	Do much more
1. Provides feedback to help improve my performance	O	O	O	O	O
2. Communicates honestly with his/her team	O	O	O	O	O
3. Provides clear direction about my work responsibilities	O	O	O	O	O
4. Executes action plans against our group's objectives	O	O	O	O	O

Provide Specific Advice for Action. A big challenge in a traditional 360 is knowing what to do with the results. Often a manager will sit with an HR professional to decipher what the respondents intended to convey and then try to translate that into an action plan. Their conclusions may be right or wrong but are always only a best guess based on their interpretation of the results.

In Screen 3, we solve that problem. The specific start, stop, or continue suggestions that respondents list are presented in the report so participants have specific actions they can immediately act on. The comments are verbatim (a fact communicated to the respondents before they complete the survey) and presented for each of the three priority questions. We do not present the comments for questions that are not one of the top three priorities. They are interesting, but not critical—a value-complexity trade-off.

Focus the Information to Make Immediate Action Possible. The heart of our survey report is a one page summary drawn from the two items we have described. Since the prioritization process gives an importance ranking for every survey question from one through thirty, we know which items are priorities. The report shows the three highest priority questions and lists the verbatim comments for improvement. By reading just the first page, the participant knows exactly which behaviors to change, in which direction, and exactly which new behaviors others want to see.

Step 3. Create Transparency and Accountability

Transparency

As with every OPTM process, we start with the assumption of total transparency and impose limitations only where absolutely necessary. For an area like 360s, which have traditionally been steeped in secrecy, this approach represents a fundamental change. In three areas, we believe transparency is especially important.

Be Open About the Process and Reasons for It. If the 360 might be used to help evaluate a leader, everyone involved in the process should understand this before starting. If they do not, they may feel misled or manipulated when they learn how their responses will be used. In your communication, you should reinforce the importance of behaviors at your company and share the watercooler maxim (people already know everybody's behaviors—the 360 is just a tool that records them).

Participants Should Widely Share Results and Action Plans. Sharing the 360 results and action plan with the respondents acknowledges that the participant heard his feedback, which encourages the respondents to keep providing it. It also makes the participant a role model for post-feedback behavior and shows that he plans to take action. If he also lists and shares the few things he plans to work on, everyone will know that he is serious about improving. If he asks them to tell him when he's *not* doing those things, they will know he is *really* serious.

Meetings to share results can be held one-on-one, and do not need to be overly formal. If the participants are not sharing results, it is a warning flag that they are potentially unwilling to acknowledge and act on the results.

Acknowledge How the Information Will Be Used. We have discussed our philosophy that 360 data should be considered when making decisions about personnel moves such as assignments and promotions. How a leader behaves is already considered in these decisions, whether implicitly or explicitly, so we prefer that data comes from a fair, consistent source like the 360. If the 360 is being used that way, it should be one data point among many that inform the decision.

Accountability

We emphasized earlier that it is difficult to encourage motivation from 360-degree feedback alone. Accountability can play a large part in ensuring that managers take action on their 360. We can drive that accountability in a number of ways.

Let Managers Know Their Careers Will Accelerate or Decelerate. Transparency about the potential impact of leaders' behaviors on their career is a driver of accountability. If they know that proper behaviors are required to advance (and which ones), they are empowered to start improving those behaviors and they understand the consequences if they do not.

Measuring Year-to-Year Progress. What gets measured gets done—it is a scientific fact! If your company is serious about behavior improvement, then hold managers accountable for annually improving their 360 scores. Ignore complaints that "different people will be evaluating me" or "I need to act tough to get this new group in line." Behaviors are remarkably consistent across jobs and situations—people won't become jerks just because they have new roles (and vice versa), and results can always be viewed in context. The consequences for improving or not improving can be varied: integrated into a performance review, tied to compensation, or simply discussed as a positive or negative influence on one's career.

Make the Process Transparent. Transparency in this process drives individual accountability. The more people who know someone's development goals, the more focused he will be on achieving them.

After the 360: Effective Follow-Up Using Daily Questions

Follow-up and accountability are the critical ingredients to ensure that 360s have impact. Traditionally, we in HR have relied on either managers or employees to take the initiative or have possibly hired an external coach. The first solution is unreliable, and the second can be expensive. Fortunately, there is a coaching alternative that is amazingly effective, costs nothing, and anyone can do. Peer coaching, designed by Andrew Thorn and Marshall Goldsmith, could easily revolutionize how people follow up on feedback.

The mere thought of peer coaching is enough to cause most leaders' hearts to race. Disclose weaknesses to peers? Ask them to help you improve? That sounds like a great way to be the topic of tomorrow's watercooler discussion. In reality, the daily questions process involves less disclosure than traditional coaching and uses Goldsmith's feed-forward methodology to keep anxiety to a minimum.

Identify a Peer Coach

Your peer coach can be anyone who is willing to work with you on the process—a trusted coworker, friend, or even a family member. The only requirement to be a coach: he or she is willing to invest five minutes a day to ask you a series of questions that you have selected. Ideally, your coach is also someone who wants to improve a behavior or two, and you can concurrently coach each other.

Identify a Behavior That You Want to Change or a Goal to Achieve

In executive coaching, we advise that you select no more than three change goals, but the daily questions process allows you to select many more. We recommend starting with two or three goals to get started and building from there over time. The behaviors or goals you select can be professional (give more timely feedback to my staff), individual (get to the gym three times a week), or even personal (attend all of my son's soccer games).

Ask for Feed-Forward

Ask a number of people for one suggestion on how to reach your goal or goals. It might be easiest to start with your friends, but you will be surprised at the valuable advice you get from anyone you ask. After you ask, just listen. Don't critique the answer, tell them you have already tried it, that it is too hard, or that you had already thought of it. Just write it down and say thank you. You can use all or none of these suggestions to achieve your goal, but it is worth carefully considering each of them.

You now have a coach, some goals, and some suggestions for how to achieve those goals. It was easy!

Choose Your Daily Questions

Each day your coach will call, e-mail, or text you the questions that you have requested. The questions should be ones that help you track whether you are making progress toward your goals. What makes the process fast and easy is that the answer to the question can only be yes, no, or a number. For example, if one of my goals is to give more timely feedback to my staff, one question might be, "Did you have an opportunity today to provide feedback or feed-forward to a staff member?" Another question might be, "Did you use that opportunity to provide feedback?"

If your goal is to get to the gym three times a week, the question could be as simple as, "Did you get to the gym today?" Create a list of those questions to give to your coach.

Make the Call

Goldsmith describes how the daily questions process works with his peer coach Jim Moore, former CLO of Sun Microsystems, Nortel, and BellSouth:

> Every day Jim asks me the same 24 questions. Every day I ask Jim the same 17 questions. Jim and I each have a spreadsheet of each other's questions where we record for each other the answers: "yes," "no," or a number. Structuring the questions in this way keeps the phone call moving. Each phone call lasts only a couple of minutes. We send each other our completed spreadsheets weekly. If we miss a day or two, we simply "catch up" later.[a]

a. Andrew Thorn, Marilyn McLeod, Marshall Goldsmith, "Peer Coaching Overview," July 22, 2009, http://www.marshallgoldsmithlibrary.com/docs/articles/Peer-Coaching-Overview.pdf.

If you are doing well, there is nothing wrong with your peer coaches offering some praise, and you should ask them (and others) for feed-forward if you are not happy with your progress.

Daily questions reflect the best of the OPTM approach. The process is simple and free, so there's no barrier to using it. There is accountability through the daily calls. There is transparency because your coach knows your goals and your progress. And we can assure you that you will reach your goals if you follow through.

In Summary: The OPTM 360 Assessment

Our recommended approach features several improvements on the typical 360-degree assessment. A focus on future behaviors, not on today's, reduces the risk of defensive reactions to feedback. An easy prioritization process identifies the three most important items to improve, allowing the manager to focus on those behaviors that matter most. Specific recommendations for improvement from those who know the manager best mean that he or she can start working immediately on those behaviors. And, as seen in figure 3-2, the report easily sums up the key information in the first two pages:

- *Prioritized behaviors for change.* The participant is focused on the three highest priority items their respondents select. Instead of attempting to determine their priorities for action from pages of charts and graphs, we simply tell them.

- *Practical and specific advice on how to change.* The participant gets verbatim suggestions from their respondents on exactly how they should change.

FIGURE 3-2

Example of OPTM 360 Report

Your 360 Development Report

What this is: You had asked your coworkers to rate which behaviors you should change and how. This report provides a summary of their responses, focusing on items that they indicated were a priority for you to change.

How to use this report:
- Read through the results, focusing on the priority questions and the suggestions for improvement.
- Identify the one or two behaviors you would like to change.
- Identify specific opportunities for when you can both practice that behavior and get feedback on it; confirm these choices with your manager.
- Ask your local human resource leader for input if needed.

Your three priority questions	Do much less	Do less	Do not change	Do more	Do much more
3. Provides clear direction to team about work responsibilities.			M	D P	
21. Develops team members by providing challenging experiences.			M	P	D
11. Partners effectively with team members outside headquarters.			PDM		

Your three priority questions	Suggestions for change
3. Provides clear direction to team about work responsibilities.	• Please be more clear with your team about their scope of work before you give them a project. They sometimes start on work that is already being done by others. • You should help your team align their activities better with the finance strategy since they seem to work on projects that are interesting but not quite as aligned with what we're trying to do. • Stop having your planning and analysis people analyze and report on information that they're not responsible for. • We like the flexibility but not sure how what we're doing ties to our bonuses.
21. Develops team members by providing challenging experiences.	• We're very busy, but we really aren't learning anything new. It would be great if you could rotate some of us into new roles so we can learn more. • Please get us assigned to some of the larger finance projects. • Your "slow and steady" mantra on career growth doesn't work for everyone. Start understanding the different career needs of your staff. • Offer up your staff more often when we need project members.

Overcoming Objections

By asking fewer questions on the 360, the leader will not get a comprehensive view of all of her leadership behaviors.

Correct. She will get a complete view of the areas that really matter. We established earlier that awareness does not lead to motivation. This means that informing a leader about areas that are not important will, at best, add needless complexity and, at worse, misdirect the leader to work on noncritical items. Awareness of how a leader compares to some comprehensive model of good leadership is interesting but irrelevant.

If you let participants know that the 360 results could have an impact on a leader's career, you will get less honest responses.

There is some evidence that when participants know the 360 is directly used for evaluation, they increase the intensity of their response, either more negative or more positive. Other research indicates that people might be more lenient if they know the survey is used in evaluation. Some studies show that if colleagues believe their feedback will negatively affect the subject, they modify their responses.[11] However, those studies typically refer to a 360 about performance, not behavior. We are not suggesting a 360 be the only tool used to evaluate behavior. In our 360 design, the suggestions are what matter most, so a less extreme rating along with a good suggestion has lots of value.

Would anyone actually choose "do much less" on your suggested scale?

We have found about 0.5 percent of all respondents choose that, and about 2 percent choose "do less." With numbers that low, you might think we would remove the choice. We keep it for two reasons. First, research shows that respondents typically do not use the extremes of any scale. By having both "do less" and "do much less," we make it easy for respondents to choose "do less" because there is a more extreme choice available. Second, there are some questions for which "do less" is the exact right answer for that person, and removing that choice eliminates the possibility that the participant receives accurate feedback.

It is fair to share a manager's 360 with others before he or she has had a chance to improve his or her behaviors?

Please refer to the watercooler maxim—the organization already knows how he or she behaves. We certainly support giving the manager fair notice about behaviors before any consequences for not changing them. We recommend that after a manager's first 360, he has a one-year period before behaviors are measured again and he is held responsible for changes. In the interim, this valuable information should be incorporated into decision-making processes where appropriate.

Assess Your 360-Degree Process

- Is your 360 process customized to the behaviors that are most important for your organization's success?

- Does it take more than ten minutes to complete?

- Are the results easily understandable by the average manager?

- After reading the 360 report, does the manager specifically know both which behaviors to change and how to change them?

4

Talent Reviews and Succession Planning

IF YOU ARE LOOKING for the engine of effective talent management, you have found it.

The talent review process helps you to understand the talent you have, identify the talent you are missing, and create plans to address both. You will know where investments in growing talent yield the best return and where it is smarter to divest. The simple OPTM process will accomplish this with a minimum of paperwork and bureaucracy.

Depending on which survey you read, between 50 percent and 75 percent of firms engage in talent reviews and succession planning; about half of those use a formal process.[1] That number seems low to us. We can understand that company executives are skeptical about conducting engagement surveys or think that there are alternatives to a typical performance management system. But to have no formal process for assessing talent or planning for succession is just irresponsible.

Talent reviews and succession planning should be the practices that are the most compelling to boards and senior teams. There have been enough untimely CEO deaths (e.g., Charlie Bell and Jim Cantalupo at McDonald's, Reginald Lewis at Beatrice Foods), and performance-driven departures (e.g., Rick Waggoner at General Motors, Chuck Prince at Citigroup) in recent corporate history to convince every board member and senior executive that planning in advance for key transitions is critical. Particularly in growing companies, "the focus is often on recruitment of key talent," says N. S. Rajan, partner and human capital and global leader, HR Advisory at Ernst & Young, "and not enough attention is given to the development of internal talent." A robust talent review process ensures a healthy balance.

By talent review process, we mean the regular cycle of evaluating a company's leaders consistently and systematically. The process has two primary objectives: to understand the quality and depth of the leaders and to plan for succession by predicting which leaders will succeed (their "potential to advance"). Some firms call this succession planning, but we believe that talent reviews are a more comprehensive process to drive investments in talent than a staid process to identify who will take someone's chair. Talent reviews should provide the information necessary to make smart succession choices and guide how the company invests in potential successors. Succession planning is a more mechanical process to identify which employees are best positioned to fill which roles, and to track whether the successor's skill and behavior gaps are being closed.

The power of talent reviews lies in their consistent, disciplined execution. Jim Shanley, former head of leadership development at Bank of America captures the concept perfectly when he says that talent practices should have a "regular corporate rhythm." We believe that if a company did nothing more than have regular discussions about talent every six months and followed up on each decision, talent quality and depth would soon eclipse the nearest competitor's. Just by using a simple tool (the performance and potential matrix) and some clear definitions about what *potential* means in your organization, you can understand your talent and best decide how to grow, challenge, recognize, and reward them.

Step 1. Start with the Science

A central goal of the talent review process is to accurately predict which employees will progress and succeed in the company over time. The more effective a company is at that task, the more likely it is to have the right talent available when and where needed. Theoretically, this process should increase a company's competitive advantage by ensuring that its most important roles are always filled with the best talent.

Unlike performance management or other talent practices, which emerged from a scientific construct, the talent review and succession process was designed for tracking and reporting. There's no science to guide the process design, and except in the area of CEO succession, no body of evidence that the outcomes of succession planning benefit the company.[2] Although we do not have proof that the integrated pieces of a talent review process work, we do know that strong research supports the effectiveness of the individual pieces.

One area in which the science is helpful is providing practical insights and direction on why some individuals consistently perform at a high level. Researchers have been interested in this topic for years, so voluminous if not totally conclusive science is available. Although there is no proof that a collection of consistently high-performing individuals will produce a consistently high-performing company, the whole is not likely to be substantially less than the sum of its parts. If that is too much of a leap of logic, we know that high performers will be maximizing results in their area of the organization.

The research on individual success suggests that there is no one secret to consistent high performance. What we know is that a few factors matter more than others.

Smart Wins Every Time

The research on general intelligence (roughly equivalent to IQ) and its impact on job performance is as compelling and conclusive as talent management science gets. Simply put, how intelligent a person is will determine her long-term job performance much more strongly than any other factor. Current research finds that it explains somewhere between 9 percent and 25 percent of differences in performance.[3] On average, a smart individual will outperform a less smart individual, in any job, in any environment. It is that clear.[4]

Maybe you believe that some people are smart in a very specific way—that someone's strong verbal abilities or quantitative skills can compensate for lower general intelligence. Might that provide some unique advantage compared to just having high intelligence? The research finds that the answer is no. General intelligence level will still be the best predictor of success, and focusing on specific aptitudes, even when they seem related to someone's job, does not provide any significant advantage.[5]

The same holds true for the impact of experience versus intelligence. While a more experienced individual will perform at a higher level than a less experienced one, particularly for the first few years on a job, that difference fades over time, with general intelligence remaining the most powerful predictor of performance.[6]

With this overwhelming evidence, why not just select talent by giving IQ tests? Although general intelligence is the largest single predictor of performance, it rarely explains more than 25 percent of the performance differential.[7] So if we relied exclusively on intelligence, we would be ignoring the majority of factors that actually explain what contributes to consistently high performance (which heavily influences someone's potential). Also, for any given job, the internal candidate pool is likely already limited to a narrow band of general intelligence. You are not trying to differentiate candidates who are smart from those who are not; you are trying to understand the finer differences among everyone who is very smart. Among highly intelligent people, differences in intelligence are not a strong predictor of performance. That increases the relative importance of the next two factors.

Some Personality Traits Matter (But Most Don't)

Research shows that general personality tests have a small, but incremental ability to predict job performance. While these results tend to be limited to specific situations or job types, the personality trait of conscientiousness (having high self-discipline, carefulness, thoroughness, organization, and so on) consistently explains variation in job performance across all job types.[8] The research varies on its exact impact, but anywhere from 5 percent to 9 percent of the differences in job performance can be attributed to differing levels of this trait.[9]

How Well Someone Fits the Company

Individuals intuitively feel if they fit with an organization. The employees seem to share their values and approach things in a similar way. It just feels natural. Interesting science in an area called person-organization fit explains these feelings and how they affect success. The underlying premise of person-organization fit is that people are likely to be more satisfied and to stay with an organization if there is a higher fit between what they value or believe in and various attributes of the organization or job. Those organizational attributes include aspects of culture, values, roles, and leaders, among others. The correlation between fit and outcomes like retention or satisfaction is modest but statistically significant, so it is worth considering fit when trying to predict an individual's long-term performance.[10] We discuss fit again in chapter 6, when we discuss competencies.

Step 2. Eliminate Complexity, Add Value

A simple, intuitive tool makes talent reviews easy for managers, but its true power comes from disciplined and regular execution. When the two elements are effectively combined, you have built a strong foundation for everything else you do in talent management. Despite simple tool and process, there is a lot to say, so we have separated the discussion into two parts—one discussing the tool and the other the process.

Eliminating Complexity

An effective talent review process uses the least amount of data necessary to make the right decisions. At more than one organization, we have seen the information required for each talent review occupy a thick binder or fill up a thumb drive. Much of this material is interesting, but keeping the process simple means understanding where each piece fits on the value-complexity curve. We discuss the tools and process that best maintain that balance next, along with practical advice for effectively managing the process.

Use the Performance and Potential (P x P) Grid. There is no better way to easily differentiate employees than by charting them on a P x P grid (see figure 4-1).

As the name implies, one axis measures performance and the other measures the leader's potential to advance in the company. If you add a few summary statements about your talent on the same page, you have captured 90 percent of the information you need for a successful talent review. According to Lucien Alziari of Avon Products, "I'm not sure you need to use much more than a nine-box performance and potential chart [in talent reviews]. It's very simple, uses definable terms, and forces people to choose and differentiate."

FIGURE 4-1

Example of Performance and Potential Grid

| | | Potential | | |
		Lowest potential rating	Middle potential rating	Highest potential rating
Performance over time	Highest	Stewart Griffin Chloe Kiton Max Kaatikoos Linda Thornton	Lui Zhang Ricardo Acelero	Joe Bobson MaryEllen Chang
	Medium	Marie-Pierre Dumas Robert Smith Alexis Watanabe Lauren DeBussy Alisa Dracon Thomas Hildon Juan-Carlos Mesia	Cristiana Gomez Charles Reilly	
	Lowest	William Schmidt		

From an OPTM standpoint, this one tool could be the ultimate combination of simplicity and value. Using it is easy to explain. Managers' accuracy with it quickly improves with practice. The administrative burden is low because the average manager can place his entire team on the grid in two minutes or less. The results allow managers to allocate their organization's development resources to where they will have the greatest impact. That combination of factors makes it a powerful tool, but one that must be used carefully. The wrong assessment of a leader's potential can do long-term damage to his career.

Keep the P x P grid simple. First determine how many different categories of performance and potential you need to measure on the P x P grid. Some grids have up to five dimensions for each measure, giving twenty-five different ways to categorize employees. Complexity certainly outweighs value in that case. The grid's primary purpose is to help differentiate investment in talent. A company is not going to have twenty-five distinct ways to invest. Three performance categories and three potential categories are sufficient; four is tolerable but of little additional value. For a potential category, the first would be some form of "well placed for now." You need to decide what time period that includes.

The next two categories are meaningful gradations of how far and how fast someone can move in the company. One way to determine that is to review the career progress of the current senior leadership team and chart how they moved through the organization. If they each moved one level every two years, you could use that to gauge the speed of movement that indicates high potential.

There is no right set of labels, but in this area, iterations are not helpful. Line managers do not want to see different potential definitions each year, and you lose the ability to track an individual's progress if you do not have consistent measurements.

Assess potential to advance. When we say *potential*, we mean potential to advance levels, in contrast with organizations that identify underlying qualities such as social intelligence, ambition, values, or other dimensions. Those dimensions are interesting but not necessarily practical. Talent reviews are a succession-planning tool, so unless potential to advance is assessed, the value of the tool is greatly diminished.

There are two approaches to determining if someone has potential to advance in an organization. One approach is to *inductively* establish criteria that describe what capabilities or qualities a high potential should have, evaluate leaders based on them, and then label anyone with those capabilities *high potential*. People who believe that high-potential assessments or fit with a detailed competency model will accurately predict who will advance in the company take this route.

In short, if someone fits the model, then by definition they have high potential in the organization.

A second approach is to *deductively* ask leaders to identify individuals they believe have high potential and then determine what criteria they used to make that choice. For example, if we say that Sue and Bob have high potential to advance (they are in box 1 in the P x P grid), we should be able to identify the few vital things that differentiate them from others who have only good potential to advance (box 2 in the grid). The few differentiating elements indicate high potential.

Many talent practitioners feel most comfortable with the inductive method. However, the deductive method is much more effective due largely to one key fact—an individual's potential can be highly situational. As we discussed in the science section, high potential is not a constant state of being. A leader in a growth business may not have the skills to be a high-potential candidate in a turnaround organization. The person who fits well with an entrepreneurial culture may find the fit in a more bureaucratic one challenging.

Alternatively, the company can adjust the leadership behavior model every few years to reflect these changes (and that might be appropriate), but it is likely that deductive talent review conversations will identify these changed requirements long before the company can formulate them into a new model. Essentially, by the time you know enough to change the competency model, it's too late for it to have an impact on the selection of high potentials for that particular environment. That is one more reason to keep that model simple and broadly applicable.

In "How to Conduct a Talent Review," we describe exactly how to run a talent review session that identifies these few, vital differentiators of high potential and how to ensure that high-potential employees compare favorably to those outside the company as well.

How to Conduct a Talent Review

The talent review calibration process ensures objective performance and potential evaluations, clear development plans, and an understanding of what high potential means in your company. A calibration meeting brings together a manager and her team members to discuss their talent. Each team member presents the performance and potential (P x P) grid he or she prepared on direct reports and briefly describes how each person is rated. Other team members contribute their opinions based on their firsthand interactions with that person. The discussion concludes after they have discussed each person, agreed on their final placement, and identified key development steps for them.

There are three basic actions in a talent review calibration meeting.

Action 1. Inform and Train Managers

Inform managers about the process. Explain to managers that the purpose of a talent review is to assess the quality and depth of their employees so they can plan for succession and differentiate how they invest in their development. Tell them you want to do that in the simplest, fairest way possible, which is why you are using the performance and potential grid—a standard tool many organizations use. You may want to provide a simple flow chart or list of the activities that are involved in the process.

Train managers in the tools and the process. Create a blank P x P template, a sample completed P x P template, and a page that defines each P x P label (see example in figure 4-1). Tell the managers that they need to place each employee on this grid, using the facts they have about performance, behaviors, career interests, and the needs of the organization. Make sure they understand that they should have facts so they can defend the ratings in the calibration meeting.

Action 2. Conduct the Calibration Meeting

Schedule a minimum of ten minutes for each individual to be discussed in the meeting.

Discuss each manager's P x P grid. Each manager presents his or her grid, briefly describing each direct report and the reasons for the rating. Next, team members state whether they agree or disagree with the rating. Anyone disagreeing gives the facts that might suggest a different rating. The group will decide together on the final rating; this is the beauty of the calibration process. Individual biases and political considerations are neutralized by incorporating multiple views on every employee.

Agree on key development activities. The group discusses one or two significant development steps for each direct report. These include anything from developing in a current role, a special project, coach, shadowing, or any other typical development activities. If there is no time to discuss this for every direct report, at least cover the high-potential and highest-performing employees.

Review the overall grid for the group. Once the group has discussed the individual grids, it should review a summary grid that lists every individual. This review allows the group to conduct the final calibration across all their direct reports and identify what differentiates those in the highest-potential box. The group compares everyone in the high-potential box to each other and confirms that each is at a relatively similar level of performance and potential. Does the group agree that all have relatively equal potential to advance?

Define "high potential" deductively. Once the group has agreed on the final placements on the grid, you can tease out the factors used to differentiate high potential and ask the managers to contrast those in the high-potential box with those who have similar performance but are one step below on potential. "Managers often perceive strong performance as potential," says P. V. Ramana Murthy, HR leader for Coca-Cola (India). This process should help crystallize the difference. Ask why those people one step lower are not in the high-potential box. Through that discussion, you should end up with a short list of factors that differentiate the absolute best talent in the department or group.

Action 3. Record and Track Progress of Development Activities

Record all development activities. While each team member is accountable for following up on direct reports' development activities, an HR leader or another responsible person should keep a master list of those activities so they can be tracked for the next meeting.

Track and provide guidance on development plans. After the talent review, the HR leader should follow up with each team member to help with the planning and execution of any development activities.

What Enables an Effective Review

An open, honest conversation is not easy, but it is essential if you want to derive value from this process. If leaders in your company have never had to discuss talent, they are going to be uncomfortable the first time through the process. Leaders might play any of the typical games at first—hiding their talented employees by using a low ranking, importing but not exporting talent, "I won't speak ill of your people if you don't about mine," letting personal relationships influence their rankings, avoiding low ratings because they are afraid of the consequences to the individual, and so on. The HR or talent leader should facilitate this discussion and challenge individuals who appear less than transparent when talking about their talent. It will take a few rounds before real transparency begins to emerge.

Another good reason to hold semiannual talent reviews is that leaders improve with practice. If you hold four discussions over two years, leaders will noticeably improve and will soon be more comfortable with open, honest conversations.

Assess performance over time. The other axis on the P x P grid measures performance, a more straightforward metric. We look at an employee's average performance over the past three years, because everyone has an occasional great or not so great year that does not indicate true abilities. You can use an average of two years, four years—whatever works best for your company. This can be a mathematical average, which takes some of the subjectivity out of the decision, or you can leave it to the manager's discretion. As we discuss later, since managers have to defend their placements to their own manager and peers, there is a natural check and balance built into the system.

Finally, decide on the performance categories (high, medium, low; top 20 percent, middle 60 percent, bottom 20 percent) to determine who should be in each row. Your choice should be guided by the actions and investments you plan for those in the various boxes (see figure 4-2). For example, if you plan to terminate the lowest performers rather than just know who the lowest 20 percent are, you might be wise to include a smaller number of employees in the lowest category.

Consider the behavior model. In your company, if how a leader behaves is important, you should use those behaviors as a screen during the talent review discussions. A leader's ability to behave consistently with an organization's values or behavior model is a great indicator of fit. However, you should consider that ability along with other variables you think are important, because it is only one indicator of potential success.

FIGURE 4-2

Example of Talent Investment Grid

		Potential		
		Lowest potential category	Middle potential category	Highest potential category
Performance	Highest performance 20%	**Compensation targets:** • Base 50th, Bonus 75th **Development investment:** • 1.5x average **Hi-po program:** No **CEO/board expos.:** Maybe **Global move:** No **Special projects:** Yes	**Compensation targets:** • Base 50th, Bonus 75th **Development investment:** • 2x average **Hi-po program:** Consider **CEO/board expos.:** Yes **Global move:** Yes **Special projects:** Yes	**Compensation targets:** • Base 60th, Bonus 90th **Development investment:** • 5x average **Hi-po program:** Yes **CEO/board expos.:** Yes **Global move:** Yes **Special projects:** Yes
	Middle performance 60%	**Compensation targets:** • Base 50th, Bonus 50th **Development investment:** • .75x average **Hi-po program:** No **CEO/board expos.:** No **Global move:** No **Special projects:** No	**Compensation targets:** • Base 50th, Bonus 50th **Development investment:** • Average **Hi-po program:** No **CEO/board expos.:** Maybe **Global move:** Consider **Special projects:** Yes	**Compensation targets:** • Base 60th, Bonus 60th **Development investment:** • 2x average **Hi-po program:** Consider **CEO/board expos.:** Yes **Global move:** Yes **Special projects:** Yes
	Lowest performance 20%	**Compensation targets:** • Base 50th, Bonus — None **Development investment:** • None without TM approval **Hi-po program:** No **CEO/board expos.:** No **Global move:** No **Special projects:** No		

Define potential against real opportunities. It is tough for someone to have the potential to move up one level in three years if there is no level above him, there are no jobs at that level that would be a fit, or he is unwilling to move to where a job is located. Managers should be able to describe the role that anyone rated with upward potential can actually move into. Debating why Mary can or cannot be the CFO in three years will yield a better outcome than having a theoretical discussion about her potential.

Use mobility as a factor in determining potential. The issue of mobility often comes up in discussions of who has the potential to move upward. Since the definition of potential to advance is to move *up* levels in the organization (remember this should be a practical succession planning tool), if people are unable to relocate to a job or meet other requirements of that higher role, then they have removed themselves from the high-potential pool.

In the real world, people have temporary restrictions on their ability to relocate. If Bob has high school–aged children who will graduate in three years and he is willing to move to London after that, he can be a high-potential candidate. If Bob had already gained his international experience and is now located in the same office as his next few potential roles, lack of mobility should not be an issue. However, if Bob says he will never move to London even though that is where every promotional opportunity for him is located, then he has self-selected out of the high-potential pool.

Use a Basic Succession Form. Showing the talent depth in your organization needn't require bringing thick black binders of information to the table. You need little information beyond how many people can be successors in a role and how far they are from being ready. Any other information should be reported and acted on as part of the talent review. If HR technology allows you to present this information in a graphic way, use what works best for your company. (See figure 4-3.)

Hold Calibration Meetings. These meetings are the most critical ingredient in a successful talent review. As we described in more detail in "How to Conduct a Talent Review," at calibration meetings, a manager and her direct reports systematically discuss each of their direct reports. The group debates and agrees on the final P x P placement for each employee and accepts responsibility for that placement. This group discussion or calibration helps neutralize any one manager's biases. The calibration discussions are also a way for the group to become more familiar with leaders they do not know and to agree on both individual and overall talent development plans.

FIGURE 4-3

Succession Planning Form

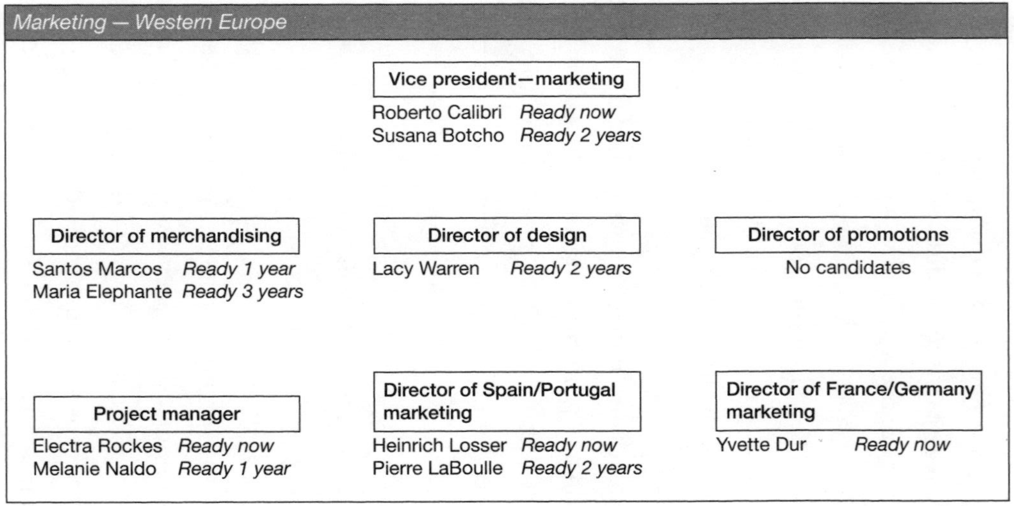

Marketing — Western Europe

Vice president—marketing

Roberto Calibri   *Ready now*
Susana Botcho   *Ready 2 years*

Director of merchandising

Santos Marcos   *Ready 1 year*
Maria Elephante   *Ready 3 years*

Director of design

Lacy Warren   *Ready 2 years*

Director of promotions

No candidates

Project manager

Electra Rockes   *Ready now*
Melanie Naldo   *Ready 1 year*

Director of Spain/Portugal marketing

Heinrich Losser   *Ready now*
Pierre LaBoulle   *Ready 2 years*

Director of France/Germany marketing

Yvette Dur   *Ready now*

You might think that calibration meetings only serve to rein in managers who overrate their team members. They can also be valuable in exposing highly talented people that a manager is trying to hold onto by not publicly recognizing them as high-potential candidates.

Review All Managerial Talent Twice a Year. If you are in a fast-paced industry where change is a constant (and who isn't?), then it seems unusual to look at employees only once each year. Talent reviews should be where you assess the talent investments you have made and whether they are paying off. Reviews hold managers accountable for having made progress on the development actions they have committed to and are an opportunity to discuss any new developmental assignments or other activities. If you have used our approach for the talent review process and reduced the time and complexity involved for your managers, asking them for a twice-a-year discussion seems reasonable.

Aggressively Manage the "Average Performance, Average Potential" Box. This topic ignites fierce debate among both line managers and HR leaders. There is nothing wrong with people being well-placed in their jobs and performing up to expectations, but they probably should not be in the same role forever. A number of negative consequences can occur. One consequence is that they block succession to other jobs. "Organizations struggle more with moving blockers than with almost any other aspect of talent management," says Allan Church, vice president of organizational and management development at PepsiCo.

Failure to remove blockers can seriously impede an organization's ability to follow through on development plans. For example, if a company's two marketing manager roles provide invaluable experience on the path to brand manager, having someone sit in that role with little potential to move up prevents the company from developing the brand managers needed. Another consequence is that the company is potentially giving up performance benefits that could help it if a superior person were in that role. The difference in performance between an average performer and one in the top decile is tremendous. By keeping an average potential and performance employee in any role, you are saying that the company is willing to sacrifice high performance for quite some time.

This sacrifice may be a wise investment if you are training a new leader, or there may be other reasons that justify it. But the choice should have specific objectives and a time limit. Are you trying to round out Mary's marketing capabilities? Which capabilities should this role help to develop and over what period of time? This does not mean that everyone is required to have high performance over time and high potential to advance. But that box labeled "middle" must be considered a nice place to visit but not a great place to live.

Track and Follow Up on Every Talent Review Decision. You have put a lot of effort into having a thorough, accurate discussion of the company's employees and how to most effectively develop and deploy them. Tracking and following up on every action item will help you get the best return on your investment. An HR or talent leader in every review should keep track of the action items discussed. He or she should confirm these items with each manager and then check for progress at the next review. In the accountability section, we discuss how to ensure that leaders are accountable for moving forward with the action items for their team members.

Just as important as what you include in your process is achieving simplicity by what you have left out. There are a few things you should not do during performance reviews.

Do Not Create Overly Detailed Individual Profiles. Using the least amount of information necessary to make the right decision helps ensure that complexity is kept out of a process. The use of employee profiles is an example of why caution is needed in including any additional piece of information in the process. An individual profile is a summary about an employee that lists information helpful to the talent review process, including job history, strengths, development needs, and so on. That information seems reasonable to include in a talent review discussion, but let's consider a profile's true value. Is it used to explain why someone is in a particular box? No, that is the manager's responsibility, and there is not enough information on the form to explain it anyway. Is it used in case others around the table do not know the person well enough? If they do not know the person well enough, they should not provide their opinion on the P x P placement grid. If they just want to get to know the person better, then send them the profile after the review, or better yet set up a meeting or call.

Do Not Create Fancy Labels or Definitions for Each Box in the P x P. Eliminate any element of a talent practice that requires translation into simpler language. The cute labels that people assign to P x P boxes certainly fall into this category. Labeling someone who has low potential and high performance a "high-impact performer" means nothing. Neither does labeling someone with high potential but low performance an "enigma" (both are real labels we found in a quick Web search).

Similarly, a one-sentence description of a particular box is at best redundant and at worst misleading. The box that indicates people of average performance and average potential is exactly that. Call it box six or nine or three if that makes it easier to remember, but do not include a sentence in the box that says, "These individuals are not likely to advance a level in the near future but have demonstrated between slightly below to slightly above average performance over time." We know that is what the box means; we can read the titles of the rows and columns. Any further definitions will emerge from the talent review discussions.

Do Not Use Standardized Tests to Predict Potential. If potential is contingent on the unique aspects of a company and its strategy, then how can one standardized assessment predict the high potential to succeed in every company? Some consulting firms sell tests that they guarantee will predict who has high potential and who does not. As we explain in the science section, this is not backed up by thorough, academic research. The best an assessment can do is separate the "wheat from the chaff," but it is not going to tell you which is the best wheat for your company. "Assessments might predict broad capability, but they will not be helpful in identifying talent for specific jobs or job categories in your organization," says PepsiCo's Allan Church. There may be some value using them to help with hiring decisions, but here they add complexity and may even guide you to the wrong decision.

Standardized tests are also a crutch, not a tool, which managers use as a substitute for making their own talent decisions. A manager's job is to know people well enough to have a point of view on their potential to advance. If you give her a crutch to lean on, she will never learn how to walk on her own.

IBM's Five-Minute Drills: Group Ownership, Disciplined Process

Talent reviews are the best way to assess potential moves for leaders, but that process can lose discipline in the time between review meetings. IBM solves that problem with its Five-Minute Drills. According to Mike Markovits, vice president of business and technical leadership, "If you're the senior vice president of a business unit and you want to move someone one level down—any of the top five hundred people at IBM—you can't take that action on your own. You need to bring your recommendation to the chairman's staff meeting, along with a description of the job and a slate of candidates." Every proposal is presented in a standard format, and what follows is a discussion among the senior leaders to decide if the move is the right one for the person and the organization. The entire process is replicated each month in every senior leader's staff meeting.

Markovits admits that despite their name, the actual discussions can take up to sixty minutes. We consider the Five-Minute Drill a great example of OPTM because it:

- Is simple to understand at any level in the organization.

- Uses a consistent process in every department.

- Has the sponsorship of the top team.

- Is light on paperwork.

- Is required for everyone.

Adding Value

The performance and potential grid adds the most value to the talent review process by summarizing complex information in an easy-to-understand format. That same format can help managers and HR understand how to invest in their employees and determine if those investments are working.

The talent review provides nine different categories of performance and potential. How a company invests in each of those categories will dictate how effectively and quickly it builds better employees. One rule is that the company should have a consistent investment philosophy for the employees in each box of the grid. Everyone in the same box does not receive the exact same investment, but there should be a narrow range. The investment should also be noticeably different than that made for the other boxes. The clearer managers are on this topic, the smarter decisions they can make about investment in their talent.

We recommend using the talent investment grid we discussed earlier, which mirrors the P x P. The grid should be the output of a discussion among the senior team and HR that determines a differentiation and investment philosophy. For example, should the investment in the highest potential talent be 50 percent more than in the average talent? 100 percent? 500 percent? The Top Companies for Leaders survey found that companies that best develop talent differentiate much more aggressively than average companies.[11] A company's approach should reinforce the business direction and culture or, if it is trying to change either of those, the new direction and desired culture.

We suggest differentiating in certain areas. (We use the term *boxes* below for ease of discussion, not to devalue the people we are talking about.)

- *Development investment.* Which boxes get first shot at the best assignments? Who is eligible for expatriate assignments? Who is selected first for important company projects? Who is selected first to attend leadership development programs? Who is eligible for external education? You do not need to have a specific guideline for each one, but you should have clarity on what you consider to be the most important investments.

- *Compensation investment.* What types of compensation should be used to differentiate, and how much differentiation should there be? The Top Companies study found interesting differences in how the top companies reward potential compared to other companies. While those companies not at the top rewarded potential more frequently using base pay and annual incentives, top companies used long-term

TABLE 4-1

How Top Companies Differentiate Their Talent Investments

In companies where compensation is linked to a leader's potential to advance, the following types of compensation are included:	Percentage of top companies	Percentage of companies not at the top
Base pay	53%	78%
Annual incentive	53%	72%
Long-term incentive	87%	53%
Stock grant	60%	28%
Stock options	100%	65%
Restricted stock	100%	44%

incentives (options, restricted stock, stock grants) much more frequently. Top companies were also more aggressive in their differentiation; 67 percent gave high-potential leaders long-term incentives valued above the eightieth percentile. Only 28 percent of companies not at the top followed a similar philosophy (see table 4-1).[12]

- *Senior team and board investment.* An executive team's time is a valuable commodity, so you should differentiate this invest-ment as carefully as any other. Who should be eligible for senior team mentoring? Who needs exposure to the board? Who should board members and executives visit as they travel around the world?

Step 3. Create Transparency and Accountability

A number of long-debated questions arise when we discuss trans-parency and accountability, from "do you tell them?" to "how can you make them follow up?" As always, we recommend a maximum amount of transparency and accountability to create the most successful process.

Transparency

Ensure That High-Potential Employees Know They Have High Potential. One outcome of a talent review discussion is that at least one person is likely to be rated a high-potential employee. What to do next seems to generate great angst among HR professionals. Jim Shanley, formerly of Bank of America, expresses this well: "In 1989, a colleague and I were lamenting going to HR conferences and hearing the 'to tell or not to tell' question. That was twenty years ago, and our profession still can't agree on this! My personal philosophy is that talent practices should be very transparent."

We do not think the question is complex and wonder why it occupies so much of the dialogue in HR. According to Ann Beatty of Psychological Associates, "Companies are afraid that if you tell someone that they're a hi po, they'll feel they're on easy street and it will be difficult to tell them if they don't remain a hi po. For those with less potential, they're concerned that if they tell them that they'll leave. Both of those fears are overblown."

The OPTM perspective is to start with 100 percent transparency of every talent practice and alter that only for an extremely strong reason. So, yes, we do believe that high potentials should understand that the company thinks they have a bright future and that the company plans a significant investment in their careers (if that is really true). Doing this effectively means managing the conversation carefully.

Discuss Commitment and Investment, Not Necessarily Labels. All employees, regardless of potential, want to know what investment their employer will make in their development. Communicating a label without a commitment does more harm than good. The conversation with a high-potential employee after a talent review should have the same content as the conversation with any other employee: "These are your strengths and development needs that we discussed, and here's what we see as potential career steps." If you don't share the actual label, a good metric for a successful conversation after a talent review is if the employee can accurately place herself on a P x P grid at the end of the discussion.

The only caveat to this advice is that, if you do not plan to significantly differentiate the experience of the high-potential employee, do not have the conversation at all. You are setting yourself up to lose high potentials quickly if you say they are terribly valuable to the company and they see nothing that proves that during the next year.

Balance the Conversation. Anyone is subject to having his ego expand if he is continuously told and treated as if he is a rock star. High-potential employees are no different. The conversation with them needs to carefully balance the benefits they will receive with the additional expectations and accountabilities to which they will be held. We structure the conversation something like this:

> Mary, I have some great feedback for you. In the executive team's talent review, everyone agreed that you have the potential to move far and fast in our company. We'd like to make a sizable investment over the next few years to continue growing your capabilities. That investment might include a global assignment, more exposure to the executive team and board, participation in our senior leadership program, and other things we feel will accelerate your development.
>
> If you'd like to take advantage of that investment, we want you to know that it will put you in a spotlight. If you succeed, more people will know about it, and it can have a significant impact on your career. The same thing will be true if

you don't succeed. This investment is in your potential, so we might increase or decrease it over time based on how we see that potential changing. It's not a permanent status. Also, even though we're telling you that you're one of our best, we expect you to manage this information with humility and maturity.

Tell Everyone Else Too. The rules that apply to high-potential employees should apply to every employee. If a person is discussed in a talent review, then she should be told the general details of that conversation. While not every word of the conversation needs to be shared, the same standard applies to all employees that applies to high potentials. By the end of the conversation, they should be able to map themselves on the P x P chart.

When we suggest this level of transparency, people typically raise a few concerns. One concern is that managers are not prepared for these types of conversations. That is probably correct, but it should not slow progress. You have a full array of choices available, from simply dictating that the conversations must happen to the thorough training of every manager. You should choose what is best for your organization, but that choice should not meaningfully delay implementing the process. Employees would probably value having a conversation, no matter the quality, over having no conversation.

Another concern is a variant of "the best people will leave because they now know they are the best." Or, "the average or low people will leave because they now know they are average or low." By being honest with them, you are empowering them to make decisions about their careers. You are now treating them like adults. You still have plenty of tools available to retain those people you want to keep.

Make All Forms and Instructions Available to Everyone. Create a transparent talent review process by sharing all your templates. Employees might ask some tough questions when they see this material, but it is better than having them guess about the process or fill in missing information on their own. The more transparent the process, the more you are showing you trust your employees.

A few years ago, Marshall Goldsmith expressed an important caveat, "Transparency and total disclosure are not the same thing." We encourage the open sharing of information, but employees do not need to know every word or every thought you have about their potential.

Accountability

Managers Must Tell Employees the Results of Talent Reviews. Clearly communicate to managers their responsibilities in the process; they should hold conversations with every employee reviewed. If you integrate the talent review process with the development planning or performance review processes, managers will need to have only one conversation.

To make bottom-up accountability work, employees should know when the reviews happen and what they should expect from their managers. A note from the CEO or business unit leader explaining the process shows their commitment. It puts managers on notice that they need to have this potentially tough conversation because not only are their employees expecting it, they are empowered to notify HR if it does not happen.

Managers Must Follow Up on Development Steps. One value of the talent review process is understanding the quality and depth of employees. That quality and depth does not change, however, unless managers follow up on the development activities agreed on in the review. "We [in HR] still need to convince some line managers that great leaders are made, not born," says American Express's Kevin Cox. This means that HR plays a pivotal role in reinforcing the need for ongoing development action. After the talent review conversation, the HR manager or talent manager should have a list of the development activities agreed on for each individual. He or she should follow up with all managers to make sure they understand their accountabilities and to offer assistance in making development happen.

At that point, the manager is officially on notice that these activities (which are added to anything else she had planned for her team members) will be tracked and reported on at the next talent review. The accountability lever here is simple: avoid embarrassment. If the CEO, department head, or local manager holds her team members accountable for these actions and asks at the next talent review whether they've completed them or not, personal pride should take care of the rest.

In Summary: The OPTM Talent Review and Succession Planning Process

Simple tools, honest discussions, and disciplined follow-up define the OPTM talent review and succession process. As seen in figure 4-4, the process eliminates extra paperwork and lengthy preparation by focusing on the performance and potential matrix as its key tool, instead of thick binders of interesting but unused information. Through a disciplined, regularly scheduled, and transparent talent review process that covers every manager, it accelerates the process of building leaders and ensures success by holding leaders accountable for execution.

FIGURE 4-4

Talent Review Form

Marketing — Western Europe

Major talent actions and why

- Franco Plage to Barcelona Centre to lead Spain In-Store Merchandising—development assignment
- Maria Suzette—Three-week project supporting OH! Cereal launch—experience on new brand launch
- Francois deBeer—Terminated for performance
- Tim DuRocher—Hired as VP design

Future talent actions, when, and why

- Yvette Dur—Promote to VP marketing Europe—Dec 2010
- Heidi Schuss—Terminate if performance doesn't improve—Dec 2010
- Henry Frittes—Get exposure to exec team to evaluate him as chief of staff—Jul 2010
- Lacy Warren—into corporate high-po program by Mar 2011

Potential for advancement

Long-term performance		(Lowest potential rating)	(Middle potential rating)	(Highest potential rating)
	High	Hans Schuler Marta Licht	Lacy Warren*	Yvette Dur
	Middle	Richard Willow* Jean-Marc Allesi Maria Siena Antonio Soliel Stephen Broadly	Fernando Toro Henry Frittes*	
	Low	Heidi Schuss		

*Rating change since last review—explain

Two key talent issues
1. ABC Co. has recruited eight marketing team members from us including a VP and two directors. It's all about pay!
2. Succession strength for director roles continues to be weak as managers are not developing as quickly as hoped.

Overcoming Objections

You cannot have a thorough talent conversation just using a P x P grid. There are not enough facts presented.

The grid is a tool that supports the conversation. Managers are responsible for coming to the meeting and being able to discuss the strengths and development needs of each of their team members. Adding additional material to the presentation does not improve the conversation. As we mentioned earlier, if the discussion participants do not know the staff member being discussed, they should not be voicing an opinion on his or her performance or potential. More paper will not be beneficial in that case. If there is a question on the facts, then it is the manager's responsibility to present or come back to the team with facts that justify the rating.

Isn't it demotivating to hear that you do not have potential?

There is a clear difference between telling someone that she might not become CEO and telling her that she has no career potential. Almost everyone has some potential at some time in some company. It does not have to be right now or at your company. And limited potential does not mean people do not have an opportunity to continue to contribute in the organization. "When communicating to B players, let them know that they are valued and they can grow," says General Mills's Kevin Wilde.

If someone believed that he could move further and faster than the current reality dictates, now is the time to tell him, no matter how this might hurt his feelings. If there is still a chance he can meet his career goal at the company, you have a chance to show him that path and re-engage him. If he is not going to reach his career goal at the company, give him a chance to succeed somewhere else.

What is wrong with having average performance and average potential? Not everyone can be an A player.

The argument is often made by academics and practitioners that an organization cannot have all A players or all high-potential employees, because it is important to have a group of employees who just loyally show up every day and do their jobs. While there is nothing wrong with being average, it is not a very stable place to be in a company. If we decide that someone else can learn substantially more in that role than the incumbent B player, the B player is going to get moved at some point (possibly out). If the role is a critical developmental experience, that average employee who is not moving up or laterally is now blocking the opportunity for someone else to be developed.

We know our talent very well. We do not need to do talent reviews because we are always reviewing our talent and making decisions on a real-time basis.

Real-time decision making is suboptimal to having a regular talent review process. How are you calibrating performance and potential? Do you understand how employee moves might affect other potential moves in the organization? Where is the group commitment to the move and the individual's success?

Assess Your Talent Review Process

- Do you have talent reviews at least twice a year?

- Are calibration discussions a part of this process at each level?

- How open and honest are the discussions at the calibration discussions?

- Are you confident that the grid ratings are correct? Too high? Too low?

- Are there clear consequences for being rated in each box?

- How well understood is the talent review process among those who don't participate?

- Are all people rated at the talent review communicated with? Are they aware of where they are on the grid?

5

Engagement and Engagement Surveys

THE RELEASE OF GALLUP'S Q12 survey instantly increased the value of employee perceptions worldwide. Gallup's claim—that a twelve-question survey could predict key business outcomes such as employee turnover, customer satisfaction, and company profitability—suggested that the Holy Grail of human resources had been found. Finally, there was quantitative proof that employees' attitudes had a measurable financial impact.[1]

The Gallup research raised awareness about engagement's potential, but the trigger of the avalanche was a 1998 *Harvard Business Review* article, "The Employee-Customer-Profit Chain at Sears." The article detailed Sears's discovery that ten items on its seventy-item employee survey could predict customer satisfaction and, ultimately, revenue.[2] Since then, corporate and consulting practitioners have identified their own examples of the engagement-profitability link. Towers Perrin's *Global Workforce Study* found that engagement resulted in increased financial performance over both one- and three-year time periods.[3] Gallup's research showed that organizations with top-quartile engagement grew earnings faster than organizations with below-average engagement. It also found that earnings per share for top-quartile organizations were 18 percent higher during the study period than for competitors.[4]

We suggest that most talent management practitioners believe that increasing engagement achieves the business objective of improving key financial and operational results. Interestingly, those in academia are far more circumspect about the entire concept; many see it as wholly developed and sold by HR consulting firms. While the processes are already well entrenched in organizations, academics now challenge practitioners to more precisely define what they mean by engagement. This seems like a worthwhile pursuit, given that a recent Society for Human Resource Management (SHRM) study found that every major consulting firm defines engagement in a meaningfully different way.[5]

Part of the engagement debate might be fueled by the different nomenclatures that practitioners and academics use. The most frequently cited definition of engagement in the academic literature is "a persistent and positive affective-motivational state of fulfillment in employees, characterized by vigor, dedication and absorption."[6] Practitioners would be unlikely to recognize that as engagement.

Other issues arise from the different processes that academics and practitioners utilize to justify their research claims. Although academics typically submit their prepublication research to a peer-reviewed journal for validation, most consulting firms are loath to release their data for independent review. Customers do not insist on peer-reviewed research, and since most consulting firms have products built around the models they propose, the back-and-forth dialogue of academic review is not helpful to them. According to John Gibbons, who leads the engagement practice at The Conference Board, "Consulting firms have their own point of view on engagement and they're not going to accept anything that contradicts those beliefs." Whether the distinctions are semantic or emerge from fundamental differences, many academics feel that the mad rush to the engagement bandwagon has led to such methodological sloppiness that we are no longer clear about what construct we are measuring.

Our viewpoint is that increasing engagement benefits the business in a multitude of ways. First, we believe that there is a causal link between engagement and business results. That data is not absolutely conclusive, but there is enough smoke to indicate that there is a fire in there somewhere. Second, there is no better way to comprehensively listen to employees and convey that you want to listen than to regularly solicit their input. Third, the data you receive (if you follow our approach) will provide managers with specific, valuable information about how to better manage their business. These points convince us that the engagement process is one of the most powerful tools you have to build a highly effective organization.

Step 1. Start with the Science

Describing the core science on engagement is challenging because, as we discussed, academics, consultants, and practitioners all disagree about its definition. However, rather than waiting for consensus, we would like to move the discussion forward by offering a simple yardstick that captures the essence of the various theories. A practical definition of engagement is "an employee is engaged if he or she is willing to go above and beyond what would typically be expected in his or her role." As shown in both academic and consulting firm studies, these "above and beyond" behaviors appear to be linked to engagement and are the ones we refer to when we use that term.

How we actually measure engagement is the next challenge. The academic literature is filled with articles discussing whether current engagement surveys actually measure employee satisfaction, commitment, or engagement, and debating what each concept means.

The difference is less significant than it initially appears for two reasons. First, we know there is cause and effect. A number of studies show links between engagement and business results, even though engagement is measured differently in each study. So if we know that engagement is correlated with performance and we know how to increase engagement, it would seem to make more sense to focus on increasing engagement than arguing about the precise definition. Also, we know that the three concepts are closely related.[7] The theoretical constructs of satisfaction, engagement, and commitment overlap heavily and yield the same types of organization benefits (e.g., retention, good behaviors, extra effort). If we pull a lever to increase any of these constructs, we are likely to increase the others.

Many Factors Affect Engagement

A wide variety of factors—the work environment, the job itself, the type of leadership, and individual personalities—influence engagement.

The Work Environment. Anyone who has sat through an undergraduate psychology class has learned about Frederick Herzberg's two-factor theory, which states that separate factors drive satisfaction (motivation factors) and dissatisfaction (hygiene factors) at work. Herzberg theorized that employees' satisfaction depends on the workplace delivering the ability to achieve results, be recognized, do interesting work, and have responsibility and opportunities for advancement. He proposed that satisfaction on these dimensions would increase one's motivation to perform.[8]

The Job Itself. The way employees' work is organized will meaningfully drive their level of internal motivation, which will contribute to engagement. This theory of job design, proposed by Richard Hackman and Greg Oldham in 1975, is a foundational element of talent management and provides practical guidance for many organizational design and organization development activities.[9] The theory tells us that the job itself may be a key factor in achieving higher engagement. This means that individual engagement is likely to be higher if employees have jobs that give them:

- The chance to use different skills

- Entire areas of work to complete, not just portions of it

- Work that they believe is meaningful

- Autonomy in how they organize their work

- Feedback about their effectiveness

Type of Leadership. Leaders can influence employee engagement in many ways. When employees feel that their leaders care about them, they are more likely to be satisfied.[10] Leaders with a transformational style (strong vision, effective communication, and so on) increase the confidence of their followers, which increases their motivation.[11] Even more powerful are charismatic leaders, those who inspire devout followers by appealing to their emotions and values. They increase engagement by "transform[ing] the nature of work by making it appear more heroic, morally correct and meaningful."[12]

Individual Personalities. Some personality traits provide a natural level of engagement, so it is easier to get certain people over the threshold into an engaged state than others. Researchers have found that various factors drive the natural engagement level, including how frequently people are in a positive mood (positive affectivity), how dedicated they are to getting things done (conscientiousness), how willing they are to shape a work environment to reflect their own preferences (proactive personality), and how much they enjoy work for the sake of work (autotelic personality).[13] Employees with higher levels of each of these traits are more likely to be engaged in almost any work environment, independent of any actions to influence their engagement.[14]

Engagement and Profitability Are Correlated

We know that engagement is highly correlated with business outcomes like customer satisfaction and profitability. Which factor drives which is the subject of intense interest, something academia is just beginning to debate. A 2002 meta-analysis examined Gallup's data covering 7,939 business units across 36 companies and concluded that "the correlation between employee engagement and business outcomes, even conservatively expressed, is meaningful from a practical perspective."[15] Some would argue that the Gallup index does not really measure engagement, but we would fall back on our earlier comments and say, "close enough."

Just one year later, another large study (thirty-five companies over eight years) found that a company's performance (earnings per share and return on assets) predicted employee satisfaction more strongly than satisfaction predicted performance. Given these mixed findings in the literature, academia seems appropriately circumspect of the engagement-drives-performance claims.

Consulting firms seem to be much more confident that engagement, independent of its definition, drives performance. A number of firms emphatically state that their engagement research proves a causal link between engagement and performance.[16] Although their results sound promising, until they release their data for independent review, you will have to make your own decision about the veracity of those claims.

In summary, academia is actively debating the precise definition and impact of engagement. While the item is important to get right, we find striking similarities in the various definitions offered and general consensus that organizations benefit when employees reach this state. Fortunately, between what the science tells us and current practice suggests, we understand the building blocks of engagement well enough to help you measure and increase engagement.

Step 2. Eliminate Complexity, Add Value

There are a few essential design guidelines for creating a simple, powerful engagement survey.

Eliminating Complexity

Ask the Fewest Questions Possible. In the OPTM approach, we always balance the amount of data we request with the value we will get from it. For engagement surveys, this means asking the fewest items possible to get the answers you need. The problem is that, until you conduct the survey and do the analysis, knowing which items are most valuable is tough. If we asked a question about every factor that science says contributes to engagement, we would have a three hundred-item survey. So where should you start?

One way to narrow the choices is to see where there is general agreement in existing research on the factors that drive engagement. A 2006 Conference Board study that reviewed twelve major engagement studies by large consulting firms found that four of the studies agreed on eight factors:[17]

- Trust and integrity—Do I believe the leaders in the organization will do the right things?

- Nature of the job—Does my work excite me?

- Line of sight to performance—Does what I do make a difference to the company?

- Career growth—Can I grow my career here?

- Pride about the company—Do I feel good about being associated with this company?

- Coworkers and team members—Do I like those who I work with?

- Employee development—Am I being developed?

- Relationship with one's manager—Do I value my manager?

By asking as few as two or three questions for each factor, you could end up with a simple but complete list of questions that drive engagement.

Ask Questions That Are Actionable. One of Gallup's Q12 survey questions is, "Do you have a best friend at work?" Although this question may help Gallup measure engagement, the average manager will have no idea what actions to take in response. Engagement questions should make taking action as easy as possible. A fair test is to ask an average manager to read each survey question and see if she can name two things she would do to improve that item if the score was low. If she answers slowly or not at all, reword the question.

Provide Data as Deep into the Organization as Possible. People can act on engagement data only if they have it, so provide survey results to the deepest organizational level possible. If the survey process is fully automated or outsourced, sharing should not be an issue. If it is manual, spend extra effort to make the survey actionable for managers.

Select (but Don't Obsess Over) a Valid Engagement Model. We have mentioned that the definition of engagement remains a slightly moving target and encouraged you to focus on "above and beyond" behaviors. To measure engagement, however, you need to put a stake in the ground about what factors you believe represent engagement. Every major consulting firm has a validated model. Do not dwell on the debate about which is right—pick one and go with it. You will be guaranteed that it will measure a meaningful portion of what is ultimately defined as engagement.

Conduct the Survey Annually. A company's managers are busy people, and they are going to focus on whatever occupies the front of their desk that day. If the last engagement survey was eighteen months or two years ago, managers are unlikely to be thinking about engagement today. If the survey was designed properly, it provides valuable information about how to better manage the business. This information is worth having at least yearly. Depending on the quality of the organization's or consultant's technology, consider pulse surveys that ask a small set of questions as a mid-year check.

The Pulse Survey Done Well

A pulse survey should be more than just a shorter, more frequently administered questionnaire. When done well, it is a highly accurate and actionable dashboard.

As Avon Products executed its turnaround plan from 2006 through 2009, employee engagement data helped to both drive actions and measure progress. Avon's managers had responded quickly to the first engagement survey in June 2006 and by early 2007 were anxious to see if their efforts were translating into results. Since they were being held personally accountable for increasing engagement, they also wanted information that would help them to quickly correct course if needed.

Avon's talent management group wanted to give managers more frequent updates on engagement progress but could not afford a full-length census survey every six months. The group members also knew that the organization would not tolerate that level of disruption during such a critical period.

Looking for a way to provide accurate information with less effort, they determined that a handful of questions within the three main engagement drivers largely influenced whether the engagement score increased or decreased. This meant that if they asked just those questions on a pulse survey, they would understand both the change in engagement and accurately see what actions were driving that change. They could then give managers the valuable, actionable information with the least amount of complexity and effort.

They created a pulse survey that included their four engagement questions and eight questions that were the strongest drivers of engagement. What managers received was a one page report that told them how their group's engagement was changing and why.

Set Quantitative Engagement Improvement Goals. Accountability for improving results lacks teeth unless there are quantitative improvement goals. Quantitative goals mean that the engagement score improves from year to year. At a minimum, everyone on the executive team should have set improvement goals for their areas. Ideally, this accountability should cascade as far down in the organization as you can measure results. In the accountability section, we discuss different ways to hold leaders responsible for improving engagement results.

As you design your survey process, a number of elements may seem very natural to include but demand a closer look. These elements either add complexity without sufficient value or are unsupported by the research.

Avoid Using Benchmark or "Norm" Comparisons. People all want to know how they compare to others. It helps satisfy their need to feel "normal." Nearly every consulting firm can provide engagement benchmarks (norms) for your industry, region, level, and so on. Two fundamental problems occur with benchmark data: it is right in only the broadest sense of the word, and it provides a false sense of accomplishment (or lack thereof).

The issue of normative data being right lies with the engagement definition issues we raised earlier and with the lack of comparability across companies and methodologies. If you do not know exactly what engagement means, you are relying on one firm's measurement of normal or average. And if you ever switch to a different survey firm, you will have the difficult task of explaining to managers why their benchmark comparisons are now different (and maybe less favorable).

The danger in a false sense of accomplishment is that people's motivation levels decrease once they have achieved a goal. Results that show a group's engagement score as equal to or higher than the norm will generate less motivation to improve than if the normative data was not shared at all. In addition, a person's response to engagement survey norms is similar to his response to unfavorable 360-degree feedback. All his defensive routines kick in to prove to others (and reinforce to himself) that either the data is wrong, not comparable to him, or correct but unavoidable given the tough choices he had to make in the last year.

The alternative to norms is actually quite simple and more motivating—continuous improvement. Hold managers accountable for a continual increase in engagement no matter what their scores are. This approach works best on a sliding scale to ensure that those starting with an engagement score of 30 percent are asked to increase scores at a faster pace than those at 80 percent. It also avoids the issue of the precise definition of engagement and takes a "more is always better" approach instead.

Do Not Report Detailed Statistics. Showing the mean, standard deviation, and other descriptive statistics is certainly the right way to show quantitative results in an academic setting. In the corporate world, using these stats implies a level of false precision (is a score of 3.49 really better than 3.42?) and is not as easily understandable as something like "percent favorable" responses. Even details that might seem basic, such as displaying the full distribution of the data on a five-point scale, can be simplified by combining them into fewer response categories.

Challenge yourself (and ask managers how) to present information in a way that will guide them to take action with the minimum level of distraction. We cover this approach in detail in the "Adding Value" section.

Do Not Rely on Focus Groups or Team Meetings to Develop the Action Plan. In an effort to be inclusive, some leaders react to engagement results by immediately seeking input from their teams on how to take action. Often, employees are delighted to respond, appreciative of the opportunity to share their suggestions. The problem with this approach is that focus groups and team meetings run the risk of pointing the leader in the wrong direction. The selected group may not be representative, there may be concerns about confidentiality, and the opinions of the most vocal members may set the agenda. These reasons are why you conducted an anonymous, statistically sound survey in the first place.

Soliciting input from employees about action plans can certainly be helpful and can send the message that the leader takes follow-up seriously. But the quantitative data should determine the action plan items. Focus groups and team meetings should instead clarify insights gained from the quantitative results or come up with specific tactics to include in the action plan.

Do Not Report Highest and Lowest Scoring Items. The highest and lowest scoring items are interesting curiosities—nothing more. Will focusing on the lowest scoring item increase engagement? Should you refrain from working on the highest scoring ones? Who knows? If the purpose of an engagement survey is to help managers make smarter decisions about their people, high and low scores serve no purpose.

Do Not Include Open-Ended Questions. One staple survey element is the open-ended question. "What other comments do you have?" or "How can we increase your engagement?" appears on thousands of surveys, and managers spend hours dutifully reading the findings and worrying about them. The survey process would be more effective if they simply threw away those answers.

Open-ended responses suffer from a number of flaws; they distract managers from the quantitative facts, suffer from selection bias, and create a potential legal hazard. Managers are distracted by the particularly poignant comments, those that relate to their particular interests and others with visceral appeal. Although the comments offer nice color commentary, managers should pay attention to the quantitative data. Why draw conclusions from comments, when the quantitative data provides reliably gathered, precise, and representative information?

Open-ended questions have an inherent bias, because the comments come only from those who choose to write comments. The research on open-ended comments in employee surveys has found that negative respondents disproportionately elect to include comments—not a very representative source for insight.[18] The debate over the value of open-ended questions is not new or specific to employee surveys. Managers see open-ended questions as a way to ensure that respondents can address an issue that may not have been an option in the closed-ended questions; some evidence supports this claim.[19] However, a well-constructed survey should not be negatively affected by this issue.

When someone comments that so-and-so is stealing or there is racial bias in department X, you now have information that requires comprehensive follow-up by HR or the ethics committee. Rather than create a pathway for anonymous snipes and legal liability, make sure the grievance or ethics process encourages people to share these comments through a more appropriate medium.

We outlined earlier what items to include in your survey, but we also want to be explicit about what not to include.

Do Not Stray from Engagement-Related Questions. The engagement survey is designed for a purpose—to measure engagement. If you load the survey with items that you are curious about, but that are not engagement drivers, you are adding complexity without value and possibly distracting managers from focusing on the most important items. Your survey provider can help avoid these types of questions. You can also conduct a regression analysis of the survey results so you can identify and eliminate questions that have little if any relationship to engagement.

Do Not Survey If You Are Not Sharing the Results. We cover this elsewhere, but reinforce the message here: if you are doing a survey and are not going to openly share the findings, stop the process now. What you are doing is about as valuable as having a 360-degree assessment that goes into a drawer. As in the 360 process, you are not hiding anything by not sharing the survey results—your employees already know how engaged or unengaged they are. They would like you to acknowledge that you know it, too.

Adding Value

Wouldn't it be great if you could tell all managers exactly how to increase engagement? You could eliminate their need to sift through thick reports, trying to understand which items have meaning and which do not. You could help them quickly focus on the most important issues and prove your value as a business partner. Employees would be thankful that their real concerns were heard through the noise. And if you believe that higher engagement means higher performance, the company would see improved business results too.

Adding value to the engagement process is the only time that our approach requires the help of statistical or survey experts, but it is worth the effort. You also need results from at least one survey administration to conduct the analysis that determines the strongest drivers of engagement in the organization. Next we outline the process for adding value and then give enough detail so you can guide a survey vendor or internal survey expert. There are three primary phases involved:

1. *Determine what drives engagement.* Understand through statistical analysis how much influence various factors in the workplace (the manager, confidence in the company, growth opportunities, and so on) have on engagement in the organization.

2. *Identify the critical questions.* Create the parameters to identify the specific questions or items that are the key drivers of engagement (using the results from phase 1).

3. *Design the report.* Design a survey report that can guide each manager on exactly which questions to address and the potential power of each to increase engagement.

1. Determine What Drives Engagement. Which factors contribute to engagement in the organization and how much do they contribute? For example, in terms of their power to drive engagement, you want to understand how "perception of immediate manager" compares to "having confidence in the company strategy" (typically a strong driver of engagement) or compensation (typically a weak driver). You can understand these relationships using a driver analysis, typically through either multiple regression or structural equation modeling (SEM). Depending on the size of the organization, you may want to look at large geographical or business units independently to see if their engagement drivers vary from the company's overall drivers. They are likely to be very similar, but any difference you find could meaningfully change the local engagement strategy.

Multiple Regression or SEM?

In practical terms, a multiple regression explains how much power each engagement factor (e.g., all questions related to your immediate manager) has to increase overall engagement, if all other dimensions are held constant. The multiple regression can tell you that the immediate manager factor is the largest contributor to engagement and that it should get more attention than other factors.

The structural equation model (SEM) gives even more insight. A SEM examines how factors interact with each other to drive engagement. In other words, you still know how much the immediate manager factor contributes to engagement, but now you also know that perceptions of confidence in senior management influence employees' perceptions of their immediate manager. This more sophisticated look allows us to truly identify the largest overall drivers of engagement.

For example, while a regression analysis may say that integrity is a primary driver of engagement, a SEM would show that perceptions of the manager significantly influence views of integrity. In that case, efforts are better directed toward improving the manager's behaviors, since these are a root cause of employees' perceptions of engagement. The SEM is our preferred choice for understanding exactly which questions or items drive engagement.

2. **Identify the Critical Items.** The information from the driver analysis enables you to produce survey reports that show managers exactly which items will have the greatest impact on their engagement score. There are several approaches. One is to focus on the dimensions found to be the key drivers of engagement and then select the specific questions that had the highest correlation with engagement for that specific work group. For example, if "confidence in company strategy" was a key driver, and the item "I understand the vision of the company" had the highest correlation with engagement in your department, you would select that as the top action item.

There are many options for fine-tuning this approach to fit your organization. For example, one risk of using only the approach outlined is that it assumes 100 percent of the population will agree on any given question, which is extraordinarily unlikely. For example, the "immediate manager" is a powerful factor, but it is nearly impossible that 100 percent of employees will rate their immediate manager as perfect on every question. The challenge is to know what the "theoretical maximum" is for any question, so you do not recommend that a manager focus on a question with little chance of upward movement.

To address that concern, one option is to combine the correlation analysis with a "potential range" analysis. You look at the lowest and highest scores on a particular item to identify the potential range of scores on that item. If the "agree" scores on "my manager gives feedback frequently" range from 35 percent to 80 percent, we would say that 80 percent is the theoretical maximum for that score at that moment. While "frequent feedback" is a great behavior to encourage, if you know that the highest score on that item is 80 percent, you should not tell a manager scoring 77 percent that he should focus there. Even though the question is highly correlated with engagement, the manager can do little to increase his score beyond that.

There are other options to consider, such as prioritizing some action items that the data indicates have a high impact on the company. This prioritization would drive consistent effort on a few critical items. Another option is to constrain items that have recently seen significant

FIGURE 5-1

Example of OPTM Engagement Survey Report

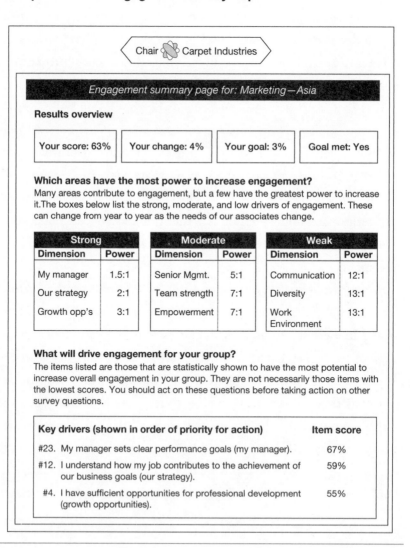

Chair 🌸 Carpet Industries

Engagement summary page for: Marketing—Asia

Results overview

| Your score: 63% | Your change: 4% | Your goal: 3% | Goal met: Yes |

Which areas have the most power to increase engagement?
Many areas contribute to engagement, but a few have the greatest power to increase it. The boxes below list the strong, moderate, and low drivers of engagement. These can change from year to year as the needs of our associates change.

Strong		Moderate		Weak	
Dimension	Power	Dimension	Power	Dimension	Power
My manager	1.5:1	Senior Mgmt.	5:1	Communication	12:1
Our strategy	2:1	Team strength	7:1	Diversity	13:1
Growth opp's	3:1	Empowerment	7:1	Work Environment	13:1

What will drive engagement for your group?
The items listed are those that are statistically shown to have the most potential to increase overall engagement in your group. They are not necessarily those items with the lowest scores. You should act on these questions before taking action on other survey questions.

Key drivers (shown in order of priority for action)	Item score
#23. My manager sets clear performance goals (my manager).	67%
#12. I understand how my job contributes to the achievement of our business goals (our strategy).	59%
#4. I have sufficient opportunities for professional development (growth opportunities).	55%

increases and might have diminished effectiveness, given the curvilin-
ear relationship between some questions and engagement. The key is to
build the appropriate formula so that the manager sees only the output—
a short list of realistic, actionable items that will have the most impact.

3. **Design Your Report.** All efforts to simplify and add value
come together on the survey report's summary page. This page tells
the manager exactly which items have the highest impact on engagement and the potential effect of each. Consistent with the OPTM
philosophy, you should design this page to show the least amount
of information necessary for a manager to make the right decisions.
(An OPTM example is shown in figure 5-1.)

Step 3. Create Transparency and Accountability

The engagement survey provides an opportunity to show your
employees that you are transparent about where engagement is strong
and where improvements are needed. Holding leaders accountable for
engagement increases (not specific levels) ensures that you extract the
true business-building value from the process.

Transparency

Share Results Openly, with Your Group and Others. As always,
our preference is 100 percent transparency, unless there is a good reason for less. Two meaningful benefits to transparency of engagement
results are: First, your employees will know that you are not afraid
to share the news—good or bad. You can also educate them about
the facts of engagement, such as level, tenure, type of job, and so on,
that can drive engagement scores. There is no reason for the folks
in sales to gloat because their scores are higher than everyone else's

(they almost always will be). Second, managers are very competitive, so use this to your advantage. If openly posted engagement scores or increases help to focus some managers on increasing theirs, it is all for the better.

Regularly Update Your Group on Survey Follow-Up. At least once a quarter, you should have formal communication on exactly what action is being taken to improve engagement. We recommend being as direct as possible, phrasing communications as "you said, we did."

Use Engagement Increases as Data Points for Evaluation. You have just gathered extensive data about the engagement of employees and what drives it. Some of that data clearly reflects managers' effectiveness. You should consider this data, or better yet, year-over-year trends, as one point of information when evaluating manager quality.

Accountability

According to The Conference Board's John Gibbons, while engagement accountability should be "drilled down to the lowest possible level," few companies hold their leaders accountable for engagement increases. He believes that many companies "still feel that the cause-and-effect relationship between a manager's activities and an engagement increase is very loose. Companies are wary to hold leaders accountable for increasing engagement until they better understand what managers can do to improve it." The benefit of the survey process we outline here is that it clarifies exactly what managers can do to increase engagement, which should make you more comfortable giving managers direct accountability for increasing engagement. There are a few ways to drive that accountability.

Embed Accountability in the Bonus or Performance Goals. We are cautious about suggesting that a company use compensation to drive accountability for talent practices, but in the case of engagement, we wholeheartedly endorse it. Few other metrics so completely capture a manager's ability to manage her team effectively. Measurement of year-over-year improvement is a fair metric on which to evaluate a manager's broad leadership abilities. We suggest using it for up to 20 percent of a manager's total bonus criteria.

Post Engagement Scores or Increases. In addition to being a key element of transparency, public posting of engagement data is an effective driver of accountability. As we mentioned earlier, managers' natural competitiveness helps to motivate them to increase engagement results. If you choose this tactic, there are three things to keep in mind:

- First, the same engagement increase in two different groups may not be equal, because groups with smaller populations can see much larger increases (or decreases) if just a few people change their minds. A group with ten members needs to have only one person move to the engaged category to increase engagement by 10 percent, while a group with a thousand members requires a hundred people to make the same shift.

- Second, employees' organizational level strongly influences their engagement scores. Those at the top of the corporate food chain (vice presidents and above) almost always have higher engagement scores than those on the shop floor. The mix of levels in each department or group significantly predicts how their score compares to others. If you post scores, be sure to explain this fact. Better yet, just report score increases, not scores, to help level the playing field.

- Third, as with 360s, managers may try to influence results through short-term actions aimed only at increasing the engagement score. We do not think you should let that dissuade you, for a few reasons. Suggesting that employees react to a radical departure in a manager's behavior by becoming more engaged does not give much credit to your employees. They are smart enough to see through short-term attempts to influence their impressions. If short-term actions do increase engagement, then we should welcome that, no matter what intent precipitated the actions. That manager will now find it more challenging to sustain or increase that level of engagement in next year's survey.

In Summary: The OPTM Engagement Survey

Our recommended approach harnesses the full power of simplicity and value to create a true business tool. We remove complexity by including the fewest items necessary to understand the key drivers of engagement. We word the survey items simply so that managers can read their report and easily understand what actions to take on their priority items. The report itself tells each manager which few items have the most power to increase engagement in his or her group. And everything the manager needs to take action is contained on one, easy-to-read page. Easy to take, easy to understand, easy to act on.

Overcoming Objections

Sounds difficult. I think I will stay with my current process.

The initial round of statistical analysis and creating a survey model can be a little complex (for you, not your clients), but is well worth the effort. Being able to tell your managers exactly which engagement items to focus on and how powerful each one is simply has no substitute. If you stay with your current model, you are missing a chance to increase your value to the business.

By allowing managers to act on questions that may have no impact on engagement, you are wasting the resources of your organization. You are also passing the analytical work over to them. Would you prefer that they spend their time interpreting engagement data or trying to increase your company's business results?

Once a year is too often. Is once every two years OK?

If the survey provides information to help better manage the business, how often would you like to have that information? With twenty-four months between each survey, engagement can go seriously off course with no indication. Busy managers also pay attention to what is on the front of their desks. The more frequently they see fresh engagement data, the more likely they are to act on it. Doing the survey less than annually suggests that it is a curiosity and not a business tool. Additionally, with the frequent movement in today's organizations, many leaders will never have the opportunity to see year-over-year results unless surveys are administered annually. This unintentionally mitigates the pressure for meaningful action to take place, and makes it even more challenging to hold the manager accountable.

If simplicity is the goal, why not just ask ten or twelve questions as some surveys do?

Simplicity that does not provide actionable data is not helpful. The survey should have just a few items to both measure engagement and understand the specific actions to improve it.

Three to five broad areas are typically identified as key drivers of engagement (immediate manager, belief in senior leadership, opportunities for development, and so on), and it takes at least three to five survey items to fully understand each. Add to that the four or five items used as the engagement index (these items create the survey score, and the key drivers are what causes these items to go up or down), and the survey is quickly at twenty items.

The ten- or twelve-item surveys that some companies offer may be great overall engagement measures, but they cannot provide the specific detail managers need to take action. With so few items, performing the statistical analysis that tells managers which questions are their priorities for action is impossible. However, ten or twelve may be the appropriate number of questions for a pulse-type survey in between full-scale surveys.

Assess Your Survey Process

- Do your survey reports tell managers the specific items that will increase engagement in their group?

- Does the senior team or CEO hold leaders accountable for increasing engagement scores?

- Does the survey take less than fifteen minutes to complete?

- Does the survey include open-ended questions?

- Is there a clear owner of the survey process—concept through follow-up?

- Are there consequences if a manager does not follow up on engagement results?

6

Competencies

OVER THE PAST THIRTY YEARS, using competencies has become universal within human resources, integrated into activities from managing performance to determining compensation. More than 90 percent of companies now have competency models, and an entire industry exists to help HR professionals create, implement, and measure them.[1] Yet their popularity belies the fact that there is significant confusion about what competencies are and almost no science showing that they work.

The confusion about competencies' meaning and value likely stems from their amorphous definition over time. After Harvard's David McClelland originally suggested competencies as an alternative to the job assessment process in 1973, they quickly evolved into a broader framework to assess, develop, and evaluate managers after the publication of Richard Boyatzis's *The Competent Manager* and Lyle and Signe Spencer's *Competence at Work*.[2] The HR community, with the encouragement of HR consulting firms, embraced the new concept and began applying it in a multitude of ways. As a result, competencies transformed from a narrowly purposed job-analysis technique to an all-purpose solution for effective performance.

These rapid changes also left the word *competency* with an *Alice in Wonderland* quality. In Lewis Carroll's classic, Humpty Dumpty explains to Alice, "When *I* use a word, it means just what I choose it to mean—neither more nor less." Competencies seem to be guided by the same logic, since popular definitions vary significantly, including the following:

- Internal characteristics of an individual that produce effective and superior performance.[3]

- A list of behavioral characteristics related to job tasks.[4]

- "A set of observable performance dimensions, including individual knowledge, skills, attitudes, and behaviors, as well as collective team, process, and organizational capabilities, that are linked to high performance, and provide the organization with sustainable competitive advantage."[5]

Competencies now appear in nearly every talent-related practice, from performance reviews to career development plans to training programs. All too frequently, they take the form of highly detailed, multilayered models that split a job or activity into the smallest possible parts. The logic is that by identifying every possible skill or behavior related to a job's performance, it is easier to develop, incent, and evaluate those activities. Our experience suggests that this level of detail, while perhaps theoretically correct, creates such complexity and adds so little value that most managers either ignore the models or can't understand them. Despite these challenges, we believe that competencies, when properly defined and applied, have incredible potential for accelerating the growth of an organization's talent.

The interpretation of competencies varies widely, so the definition we use in this chapter is "the few common behaviors in an organization that contribute to its competitive advantage." This definition is purposefully broader and at a higher organizational level than most. We believe that the demonstration of broadly applicable behaviors, rather than job-specific ones, yields true value.

Step 1. Start with the Science

The academic community is circumspect about competencies' legitimacy as an addition to the manager's toolbox. A group of researchers even stated that "most managerial competency models suffer from grave shortcomings and, at best, add little value to the performance of organisations."[6] Yet those three academics are among the few who have even explored the area of competencies. Given the popularity of competency modeling in organizations, there is shockingly little academic research on the topic. This skepticism and historic lack of interest likely stem from two factors.

First, unlike the other talent management practices we have discussed, competencies did not emerge from an academic framework. Although many other HR practices moved from a well-developed body of research into the business arena, competencies were triggered by McClelland's writings but were popularized by Hay-McBer Associates and other HR consulting firms. There was no thorough body of research then or now to define competencies or to support the numerous claims about their benefits. In fact, many academics challenge the validity of competencies as an independent, measurable construct, and find inherent contradictions in how consultants define and measure them.[7]

Second, many academics believe research conducted in areas like job analysis and leadership overlap with what many HR practitioners refer to as competencies. They see little reason to spend time studying an amorphous concept when other concrete and well-proven constructs already exist.

Regardless of the merits of this debate, there is strong evidence that one aspect of competencies—a manager's behaviors—has an impact on both individual and organization performance. And, importantly, there is also strong evidence that these behaviors can be changed.

Leadership Competencies Can Affect Individual Performance

Over the last fifty years, assessment research has consistently shown that a small group of individual factors predict leadership performance.[8] These factors are consistent with many of the leadership competencies described by the prominent competency consulting firms like Lominger, Hay-McBer, and Personnel Decisions International. So a reasonable conclusion is that these factors, such as innovation, drive, and so on, link with individual performance, whether we choose to call them leadership dimensions, competencies, or anything else.

Leadership Competencies Can Affect Organization Performance

Even more important than knowing that managers' behaviors affect their own performance is knowing that managers' behaviors affect the organization's performance, in a number of ways. Research on CEOs shows that their personalities influence top-team effectiveness and that the top team's effectiveness influences the organization's performance.[9] Managers' behaviors also affect performance when they create satisfied or dissatisfied employees. Research reveals that employees' satisfaction with their managers (a component of engagement) is related to various measures of business unit performance. The research only shows correlation, not causality, but with the plethora of studies indicating that engagement is a leading predictor of organizational performance, the relationship is likely meaningful.[10]

Competencies Can Be Developed Over Time

Studies on emotional intelligence, social intelligence, and organizational citizenship behavior suggest that people can change their behaviors, self-image, and cognitive processes in a way that affects job outcomes.[11] Put more simply, people are in control of their own behaviors and, with the right combination of incentives and disincentives, can align them with what the organization needs. Score one point for the "leaders are made, not born" side.

Competitive Advantage Can Occur When Competencies Are Consistently Demonstrated Across the Organization

This concept seems intuitive; we believe that it is true but have no hard science yet to prove it. It has been the topic of considerable research in the corporate strategy field and is a logical extension of the "competencies drive results" argument. Originally popularized by the *Harvard Business Review* article, "Core Competence of the Corporation," by Gary Hamel and C. K. Prahalad, the theory states that an organization can obtain a competitive advantage if it possesses a unique bundle of skills and behaviors.[12] Think of that bundle as thousands of individuals consistently displaying a small set of behaviors. In theory, if these behaviors result in capability the marketplace values, an organization that consistently demonstrates those behaviors will have an advantage over a competitor that does not.

Creating these bundles of behaviors should be the focus of competency-building activities in corporations. Successfully developing these capabilities can not only provide the marketplace benefits that Hamel, Prahalad, and others suggest, but also increase the internal efficiency of the organization. In every organization, common behaviors help define its culture and direct how work gets done.

These behaviors make a business more internally efficient by ensuring that work is executed in a consistent way (i.e., thoroughly, creatively, without bureaucracy), making interactions more predictable through widely known rules and providing guidance for the type of people to hire, fire, or promote. We think of this as the "coordination effect" of competencies, and, even if the larger organizational benefits cited by Hamel and Prahalad are not realized, this coordination effect provides strong justification for developing a few differentiating competencies.

Step 2. Eliminate Complexity, Add Value

The science is clear that competencies can increase both individual and company performance, but our experience has shown that this occurs all too infrequently. Although companies are making tremendous investments in designing highly detailed and complex models, they are not getting much return on that investment. One challenge is to the ability to effectively integrate competencies into other talent practices. A 2009 Towers Perrin study, *Managing Talent in Tough Times*, found only 33 percent of companies integrating competencies into their other talent practices, a number similar to the 44 percent found by a New Talent Management Network survey.[13] The power to align managers on a few critical behaviors is severely diminished each time a talent practice fails to reinforce those behaviors.

The competency models themselves are often a major contributor to their ineffectiveness. Many models suffer from having both too many behaviors and overly complex definitions. Corporate competency models with thirty, forty, or fifty separate behaviors that leaders should engage in are not uncommon. While you might think all that complexity would lead to greater uniqueness, the result is usually the opposite.

The dirty little secret of competency models is that they are all pretty much the same. You may spend millions of dollars and months of time developing one for your company, but the behaviors it describes will be among those already proven to increase organizational performance. "Around 70 percent of the competencies we see in leadership models are the same across different organizations," says Dr. Robert Lefton, founder of Psychological Associates, one of the world's top assessment consultancies. It makes sense when you think about it. A company has only so many ways to succeed, so it is unlikely that your model for success will differ substantially from your competitor's. But if the behaviors that are important in your organization are the same as the ones valued by your competitors, is it possible to create any competitive advantage through competencies? Fortunately, yes—with a simpler model, complete integration, and flawless execution.

Eliminating Complexity

Identify the Few Behaviors That Differentiate. One popular framework has sixty-seven competencies, showing that there are many different ways that leaders can behave at work. However, a few probably capture the largest differentiators of success in your business. The most important step in making competencies a source of competitive advantage is to identify the three to five behaviors from among the hundreds of possible choices. It may be easier than you think. Mary Eckenrod, vice president of talent management of Research In Motion, describes her experience at Cisco Systems: "We built a simple model with three components— 'Grow the Business, Grow Our Team, and Grow Yourself.' At that time, each of these was a critical area of focus identified by the business. The culture dictated simplicity and speed, so only three or four observable behaviors were identified for each component."

Getting to that level of simplicity took considerable effort, but it can be done.

We present two different processes to create a competency model—executive interviews (discussed next) and the OPTM Competency Matrix (discussed in the "Adding Value" section). They can be used individually or together to create a highly tailored, actionable set of behaviors.

Conduct Executive Interviews. You likely have considerable experience conducting executive interviews, so rather than providing a primer on that topic, we focus below on specific steps designed to make the competency interview productive and practical:

- *Prepare for the interview.* Learn about your company's strategy before conducting the interviews. If your company has a strategy group, start there. Ask the group members to share any documents that detail the company's strategy. Ask to interview them as well. If there is no strategy group or if the strategy is not well communicated inside the organization, the next place to go is the investor relations Web page. Many companies post their presentations to stock analysts; these presentations often contain thorough reviews of the company's strategy and progress. Even privately held companies regularly post this information.

- *Develop a point of view.* Based on your research and knowledge of your company, develop a point of view about which competencies are most important. You should be able to state which few behaviors you think are most important and why. This viewpoint should help you ask more probing, follow-up interview questions, for example, "How does our increased focus on emerging markets influence your thinking about important behaviors?"

Interview for results.

- *Ask two simple questions.* The best way to start a competency interview (after giving the executive some context for the discussion) is to say, "Describe the successful future leader at [company]. In what ways will that leader be similar to and different from today's most successful leaders?" Stop probing after you have listed four or five major behaviors. Your goal is to identify the behaviors that executive perceives to be most important, not to index every valued behavior.

- *Push for behaviors.* Executives are not expected to be experts at describing competencies, so you need to push them to specifically describe the behaviors. A great question to ask is, "What will people see when a leader is demonstrating that behavior successfully?"

- *Prioritize the results.* When you feel that you have heard the most important behaviors, ask the executive to rank the top three behaviors she has mentioned. She can use whatever criteria make sense. Your goal is simply to understand which are most important.

- *Identify the themes.* After the interviews, you need to extract the key themes and transform them into a draft list of competencies. Highlight the top priorities for each leader and list them. Group those that are nearly identical and others that are variations on the same theme (e.g., entrepreneurial, self-starter, ownership mentality). Which are most commonly mentioned? Which seem to best represent the spirit of what you heard? Which are really company-specific behaviors that can help create competitive advantage? Ideally, a few emerge as the most compelling. If not, you need another round of conversations with the executives to narrow the list.

Once you understand the few vital behaviors, the next task is to package them in a way that resonates with the organization. This step may appear to be no more than window dressing, but is critical to effective communication and execution. If the competencies are intuitive, described crisply, and sound like your organization, the chance of them being used increases significantly.

Create Short, Intuitive, Inspirational Descriptions. The ideal competency description brings behaviors alive and makes them relevant to leaders. GE has excelled at this for many years, using its values statement as its competency model. Its previous competency model included things like, "Have a passion for excellence and hate bureaucracy." To a leader, that phrase is both inspiring and exceptionally clear. GE's value model, announced in 2003, took a hybrid approach, stating eight values and aligning an action statement with every two of those. One action was, "We are a meritocracy that leads through learning, inclusiveness and change." Maybe not quite as inspiring as the previous one, but very clear in what it is asking leaders to do. GE's current Growth Values retain this simple phrasing and are incorporated in how leaders' performance is measured (see figure 6-1).

Using intuitive, simple language will go a long way toward helping managers understand and adopt these behaviors. If you phrase the desired behaviors the way GE has, you will make it easy for managers to read them, understand them, and exhibit them. If you say that they should "constructively develop their team through fostering a spirit of inclusiveness and respect," it will take them quite a bit longer to figure out what to do. They will need to ask HR, guess at what you want or, more likely, they will just do nothing.

Describe the Competencies in Language Used in Your Company. "Don't use language that makes it sound like an HR

FIGURE 6-1

General Electric's Growth Values

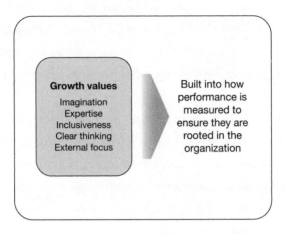

Source: GE.

model," says General Mills's Kevin Wilde. "Use the business's model with their language." The more your language and phrasing sound like those your company uses, the more likely leaders are to identify with the descriptions. Ask executives to describe the behaviors to you the same way they would discuss them with their employees. Capture that phrasing and spirit when you create the model of competencies.

Make the Competency Descriptions Applicable to All Managers or Leaders. As we mentioned, all leaders or managers should be held accountable for the same behaviors. Write competency descriptions so that all levels of managers can see how the descriptions apply to them. Using different descriptions for each level of management does not pass the complexity-value trade-off test.

Integrate the Competencies into All Processes. HR and talent leaders searching for a magic bullet to increase company performance should look here first. The 2009 *State of Talent Management* survey by the New Talent Management Network found a direct correlation between organizations that rated their talent systems as effective and those that believed their systems were aligned around a common competency model (see figure 6-2).[14] Competencies should be integrated into the performance management process, talent reviews, 360s, orientation, recruiting, selection, learning and development, and every other process than can reinforce the message that these are the most important behaviors for employees.

The forms in tables 6-1 and 6-2 enable you to do a quick audit of how effectively your company's competencies are integrated into its talent practices. Create a similar grid listing every talent practice in the organization and the competencies in the leadership model. Record specifically how the competencies are incorporated into each practice or process. This quick audit will uncover exactly where the competencies can add more value.

FIGURE 6-2

Integrated Talent Management Systems Are More Effective

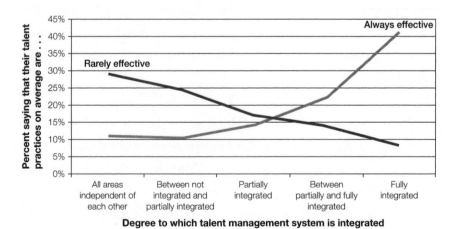

Degree to which talent management system is integrated

TABLE 6-1

How Is Each Competency Integrated into Your Talent Practices?

	Competency 1	Competency 2	Competency 3
Talent reviews			
360s			
Performance reviews			
Leadership training			
Coaching			
Engagement survey			
External selection			
Annual bonus			
Long-term incentives			

TABLE 6-2

How Is Each Competency Integrated into Your Talent Practices?

	Competency 1	Competency 2	Competency 3
Talent reviews			
360s	Measured directly		Measured indirectly
Performance reviews	Included	Included	
Leadership training			
Coaching	Up to coach to decide	Up to coach to decide	Up to coach to decide
Engagement survey	In question 4	In questions 8, 12, 18	
External selection		Included in interview guide	Included in interview guide
Annual bonus		Manager's discretion to include	
Long-term incentives	Included		

Modify the Competencies Regularly. If the competencies reflect your organization's business strategy, they should change when it does. Ann Beatty of Psychological Associates says that "willingness to change is important. OD functions get so involved in what they build that they can't imagine changing them." We have heard HR leaders offer many different reasons for not wanting to change their models: "We just finished it." "We can't afford it." "We'll have to change everything else if we do that." If competencies are supposed to build leaders who fit with the strategy, then these excuses say that the company would rather have leaders who do not fit the strategy than find a way to change the model.

Avoid Detailed Job-Level Models. If competency models can help align leadership behaviors, why not use them to provide detailed guidance on how to excel in every position? You would need solid evidence that providing such detail has a strong impact on performance to justify the resources to develop the models and the time for employees to become familiar with them. The current research does not come close to demonstrating such a link. Some research indicates that such a micro-analysis of jobs is often counterproductive, resulting in kitchen-sink models that are equally predictive of performance in multiple jobs, instead of the one they supposedly target.[15]

Adding Value

Executive interviews are a way to identify an organization's critical competencies, but we have created a tool that can serve as an even simpler alternative. In situations where the organization has gone through recent business or senior leadership changes, this approach can also be a high-value complement to the interview process that drives alignment among disparate perspectives.

The OPTM Competency Matrix. This new tool allows leaders to quickly and accurately identify a few vital competencies that will drive high performance in the company. Even better, it allows you to evaluate the leaders against those competencies and understand their capacity to change those behaviors.

The matrix identifies competencies by using one of the best understood and thoroughly proven concepts in organization science— person-organization fit.[16] According to this theory, people are more likely to succeed when they "fit" with certain aspects of their organization, which can include the culture, the business strategy, values, and so on. The better the fit, the higher an individual's performance will be (among other benefits). So how can we determine if someone fits?

Two factors best describe how a leader fits with an organization:

1. *Fit with Competitive Advantage.* How a leader's capabilities and behaviors match what is needed to achieve competitive advantage for the organization.

2. *Fit with Organizational Stability.* How a leader's capabilities and behaviors match with the significance of the issues facing the organization.

Fit with Source of Competitive Advantage. Organizations can derive their competitive advantage from many sources. Strategists like Michael Porter have proposed that cost leadership, differentiation, and focus can each create that advantage.[17] Other researchers have suggested a resource-based view of strategy, in which firms gain competitive advantage by accumulating scarce resources and capabilities.[18] The resource-based view is at the heart of the Hamel and Prahalad work mentioned earlier.

We believe that a blending of those two perspectives, where unique bundles of behaviors and skills allow a firm to be a cost leader, differentiator, and so on, are at the heart of competitive advantage. Organizations achieve that advantage by being superior at either efficiency or innovation, as shown in figure 6-3.

A firm seeking advantage from innovation would focus on being first to market with new technology, new products, or new designs. It would pursue premium pricing and large margins, trying to extract the higher returns that true innovation should deliver. An example of a firm that competes on innovation is Apple. Although it is not always a product leader (e.g., MP3 players existed years before the iPod was released), its innovative product designs and interfaces (e.g., iPhone, iTunes) provide competitive advantage that distances it from competitors.

At the other end of the scale, firms seek competitive advantage through efficiency. A firm competing through efficiency is going to organize itself to be the low-cost leader by focusing on innovative financial structures (e.g., Dell receives a customer's payment before it purchases the supplies to build the computer), innovative logistical arrangements (e.g., Walmart integrates its supply chain processes with its suppliers to ensure perfect inventory control), or more traditional cost-control models (e.g., outsourcing to countries with low costs).

A firm can certainly have a dominant innovation focus along with some efficiency (and vice versa), but a firm would find it difficult to

FIGURE 6-3

Competitive Advantage Scale

Source of competitive advantage	
Efficiency ———————————— Innovation	
Advantage achieved from efficiency of products or services (lower cost, faster, more precise, etc.)	Advantage achieved from creating differentiating products or services (novel, tailored, breakthrough, etc.)

successfully pursue more than one source of competitive advantage. To do that would require building superior capabilities in both areas, an expensive proposition. So while all firms can be represented at some point on the efficiency-innovation scale, they will more likely be toward the end rather than at the center.

The competitive advantage scale is relevant for assessing leaders because a leader's career experiences and personality type strongly influences how she fits with her company's competitive environment. We do not have space here to expound on the entirety of personality research, but we can say that personality drives many behaviors and hence significantly influences whether a person fits with an organization. Those who appreciate an environment of creativity, love change, value flexibility, are sales- and marketing-oriented, and seek risk fit better and feel more engaged in a company whose competitive advantage is innovation. Those who love process efficiency, analytics, and structure and are more financially oriented, among other characteristics, have their best fit and performance in an organization whose competitive advantage is efficiency.

Fit with Organizational Stability. Although your organization may seem as if it is in a constant state of turmoil, there are times when it is likely more stable or less stable. In each of those states, different leadership behaviors fit with what is needed to successfully manage the organization.[19] Our organizational stability scale runs from stable to unstable (see figure 6-4). We define unstable as the likelihood that an organization will face multiple significant shifts related to structural, competitive, or financial issues. A stable organization means that either minor or no issues exist in those areas. Between those two anchors is a spot for every organization.

A current example of instability is General Motors, which has just emerged from bankruptcy as a fundamentally different organization and faces huge competitive challenges. ExxonMobil represents

FIGURE 6-4

Stability Scale

Degree of organization stability	
Stable ——————————— Unstable	
The organization faces few or no significant shifts related to structural, competitive, or financial issues.	The organization faces multiple, significant shifts related to structural, competitive, or financial issues.

stability. Certainly not a business without challenges, its ability to continue finding, extracting, and selling petroleum products does not appear to be in immediate danger.

Certain leaders thrive in unstable environments. They are likely to be more charismatic, better communicators, and more strategic than the typical leader.[20] Other leaders may be more effective in an environment of high stability. They are great day-to-day managers of the business—managing projects, growing their team, and delivering results—but would not excel if asked to lead the organization through uncertain times.

Each of these characteristics is driven by personality and life experiences, so they are not likely to change in the short term. Each leader fits at and will be most successful at some point on the continuum.[21]

Use the Matrix. By combining the two dimensions, you will see that your business or business unit can be in one of four unique situations (shown in figure 6-5). In each situation, a different placement on the competitive advantage and organization stability scales defines the behaviors required to succeed. The actual behaviors to focus on are a blend of two of the boxes, depending on where you map your organization.

FIGURE 6-5

The OPTM Competency Matrix

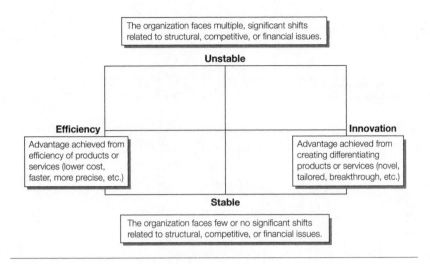

The organization faces multiple, significant shifts related to structural, competitive, or financial issues.

Unstable

Efficiency

Advantage achieved from efficiency of products or services (lower cost, faster, more precise, etc.)

Innovation

Advantage achieved from creating differentiating products or services (novel, tailored, breakthrough, etc.)

Stable

The organization faces few or no significant shifts related to structural, competitive, or financial issues.

Any organization or leader can be mapped on the competency matrix. Involving leaders in this process ensures they buy into the final product. A powerful way to use the competency matrix is to map where your organization is today and where you think it will be in two to four years. You can map the entire organization or just a single business unit. Where the organization is on the two dimensions captures today's needs and shows the distance between the current reality and future goals.

To map the organization—either at a leadership meeting or with individual leaders—show a blank competency matrix and explain the dimensions. Ask participants to place a dot on the grid that shows where the organization is today and an X where they believe it will be in two to four years (see figure 6-6). The placement of the X (or the average placement of the Xs in a group setting) indicates the range of behaviors to consider for the competency model. The distance

FIGURE 6-6

Identifying Competencies for the Future

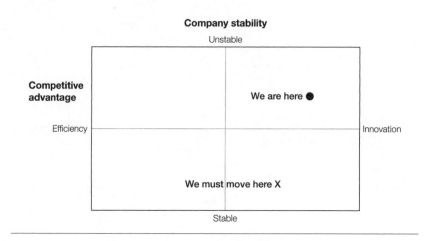

between the dot and the X indicates how much leaders' behaviors have to change to ensure the organization's future success. The greater the distance, the greater the risk that current leaders might be unable to make the journey.

Use this mapping exercise to determine which competencies to focus on. For example, if the X is in the upper right (innovation/unstable), you will want a blend of those two behaviors. If it is in the lower left, a blend of efficiency and stable behaviors is needed. We have shown some preliminary behavior ideas in figure 6-7. You can build your own competencies using these as indicators of what the correct direction is.

Once you have mapped the behaviors, you can integrate them into your HR processes so that every process that can change and reinforce behaviors is focused on these vital few.

Assessing Leaders. The competency matrix adds particular value because it supports a quick assessment of how leaders fit with the organization's needs. "Talent is not generic," says Avon's Lucien

FIGURE 6-7

Possible Competency Behaviors

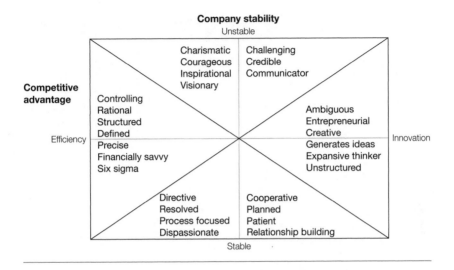

Alziari. "The definition of talent in an organization is guided by the business and the strategy." Once you understand the organization's placement on the grid, you can conduct the same mapping exercise for leaders using the list of starter competencies.

For example, which set of competitive advantage behaviors best describes Sue in marketing—those related to efficiency or those related to innovation? Make a mark on the scale to indicate Sue's balance of those behaviors. Conduct the same analysis using the stability scale. Is Sue a great communicator with a clear vision or more calm and process-focused in her work? Mark the combination of your two ratings on the grid (see figure 6-8). In general, does this describe Sue? How far is Sue's mark from the one that indicates the future direction of the organization? The greater the distance between the two, the less likely she will be a strong fit in that future scenario and the more challenging it will be for her to succeed without significantly altering her behaviors.

FIGURE 6-8

Assessing Leaders Against Competency Behaviors

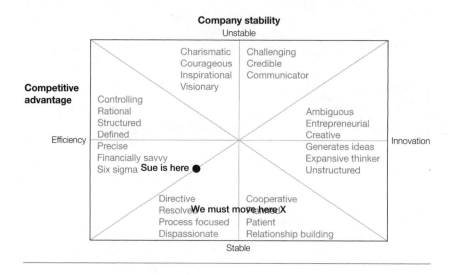

Step 3. Create Transparency and Accountability

Transparency

Competencies rarely have transparency issues, but a few points are worth highlighting. Broadly communicate the competencies, of course, and help employees to understand exactly how you use them. Are competencies used for evaluating performance? Using what tool or process? Are they included in performance management or talent reviews? If so, it is important to articulate how this works as well as the potential consequences. Full transparency means making these answers easily available on the intranet site or through other easily accessible communications channels. Managers should also understand the process and the intent behind it.

Accountability

If you are confident that the competencies you have identified are linked to superior performance, hold managers and employees accountable for displaying them. The engagement survey and 360-degree assessment are the two best measures of competency performance, and the talent review and performance management process are the two best places to hold people accountable.

Measure as a Part of Talent Reviews. Consider a leader's behaviors when making decisions about a new assignment, project, or promotion. How formally you incorporate these into the talent review discussion is up to you. You may want to have a summary of a leader's 360-degree assessment results in your proverbial back pocket. Leaders should know, of course, that their 360s will be used this way.

Measure as a Part of Performance Reviews. If you hold talent reviews and performance reviews separately, you can use them as a place to enforce accountability for behaviors. As we mentioned in the performance review chapter, whether you formally or informally measure competencies in that process, the right leadership behaviors need to be reinforced for success in the company.

In Summary: The OPTM Competency Model

The OPTM competency model has a few critical behaviors that align employees with the values or strategy of the company (see figure 6-9 for an example). These behaviors are inspirational, practical, and understandable at all levels of the organization. They are fully integrated into how you select, develop, assess, and reward people. They are clear and do not read as if designed "to be all things to all people," by a committee, or under direction of your legal counsel. They are the same at all levels of your organization and, when demonstrated consistently, create a competitive advantage.

FIGURE 6-9

The OPTM Competency Model

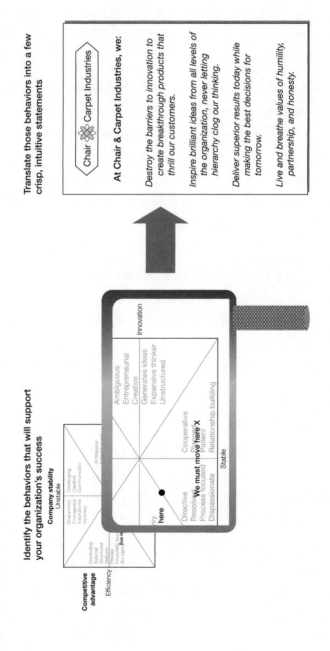

Overcoming Objections

Leaders will better understand which behaviors to demonstrate if we provide them with more detail.

Writing competencies in simple, intuitive language makes it easy for a leader to determine the right actions to take. One issue to consider is the level of risk involved in not providing leaders with a lot of extra detail. Would their behaviors be completely off the mark or still in the correct direction? With a well-written competency description, the risks should be low. If some additional detail has high value in your organization's culture, develop a one page sheet that lists a few examples of each behavior. But those examples do not need to be formally included in the competency definition. Remember that the more complex the model, the less likely it is a leader is going to understand and use it.

How can you describe career paths without a detailed competency model?

Companies discussed careers for many years before the creation of competency models, so there are other options. Careers are also not as linear as they previously were, so a career conversation should likely center on which experiences employees need to advance, not which job should be next on their list. If they are gaining the right experiences, the right jobs will follow.

This broader discussion will allow employees to think about the types of projects, exposure, coaching, and other development tools they can use to develop their skills. We suggest that conversation starts by identifying a role or two that employees might be interested in two career steps from where they are today. Map out the experiences and behaviors that qualify someone for that job, using traditional job descriptions.

Identify the various ways employees can obtain those experiences and how closely employees' behaviors match those ideal for the position. You have just done a basic development plan that should help employees take the next steps on their career paths.

We use our competency model for selection. How can we use the "pithy little statements" that you say are better than competencies?

The way you express the critical behaviors to your employees should be in the format and tone we described earlier. You can still translate them into more specific behavioral descriptions if you want to integrate them into a selection or evaluation process. Even in that case, we suggest you keep them simple and understandable. You want to ensure this does not lead to the development of a "shadow" competency model with greater complexity that will only confuse employees.

Restricting a competency model to just a few behaviors is not going to help leaders understand everything required to be successful.

It will help them to understand the most important behaviors—those that you have determined most closely link to success in your organization. By definition, if the behavior is not mentioned in the model, it is not a critical behavior. There may be interest in exploring other generic leadership behaviors in your leadership development programs. While that may be useful in some circumstances, these capabilities or behaviors are secondary for succeeding in your company.

Assess Your Competency Modeling Processes

- Can you show how each competency directly supports your business goals?

- Would your leaders say that each competency or behavior statement is intuitive and easy to understand the first time they read it?

- Are the competencies written in language that sounds like that used in your company?

- Do you have more than five major behaviors you expect leaders to display?

- Do you have more than two or three behavioral examples for each competency?

- Are your competencies integrated into your selection process? Assessments or 360s? Training courses? Performance management?

7

Sustaining One Page Talent Management

B Y NOW, WE HOPE you are an OPTM advocate. You have
started thinking through the design of every talent practice,
identifying opportunities to remove complexity, and creating
new ways to add value. Your competency model is on its way to being
75 percent thinner. You are actually looking forward to performance
reviews, so your company can see the progress you have made.

Although transforming complex, low-value talent processes into
models of OPTM is a critical first step, achieving sustainable success
requires much more. Sustainable success means that talent practices
are performing as designed, with sponsorship from the organization
and with no complexity creeping back in. After speaking with leaders from high-performing organizations like IBM, American Express,
PepsiCo, Avon Products, and General Mills, we found that three pivotal factors emerged in ensuring long-term success:

- The support of the CEO and senior team

- The avoidance of complexity creep

- The right talent managing talent management

These factors require ongoing effort and attention. Together they put the "sustainable" in sustainable talent management.

Support of the CEO and Senior Team

As any talent practitioner can testify, the difference between a CEO who understands the importance of talent and one who does not is often the difference between sustained success and talent processes that fade over time. When CEOs personally model the right behaviors—holding regular talent reviews, teaching in leadership courses, doing performance reviews on time—they send the organization a clear signal that these activities are important. When CEOs are also willing to hold leaders accountable for growing great talent, the organization is well on its way to being a talent factory.

However, having a yet-to-be-converted CEO or executive team does not preclude anyone from building a talent factory. A fundamental piece of the talent manager's role is having the credibility and courage to convince executives to support the talent strategy. According to DeAnne Aguirre at Booz & Co., "Many business leaders feel insecure about HR topics, so they avoid them and focus instead on areas where they know they'll be successful. We in HR haven't done enough to help them understand how these things work."

We have found some approaches that can be particularly compelling to skeptical executives, including financial appeal, personal appeal, and competitive appeal.

Financial Appeal

To convince certain leaders to invest in talent-building practices requires a strong financial case showing a clear, monetary payback.

That is a high hurdle for most talent practices, and making your argument persuasive requires a realistic financial assessment of the benefits. One approach is to use an actual company example that suggests a fast and real return on investment:

> Last year, we delayed starting our business in Country X because we didn't have the right general manager available. The three-month delay meant $30 million in lost revenue ($5 million a month for six months). We will face the same situation in Country Y this year and Country Z next year unless we can develop our better general managers, faster. If we can develop just two more general managers a year, we could start $5 million to $10 million in revenue flow up to six months earlier. This would help provide the cash you need for Project Q earlier than you had hoped. Here's our proposal to increase general manager strength. It will cost less than 5 percent of that new revenue.

Another method is to describe an issue that you know the executive agrees with: "Robert really needs to manage his team better if we ever hope to get Factory X up to full capacity." Ask the executive what he would pay if he could wave a magic wand and instantly correct Robert's behaviors. Propose a solution that costs half that number.

Some practices just do not lend themselves to easy financial analysis. The return on leadership training? We will never really be able to calculate a precise figure, and gyrations trying to demonstrate that one exists can become time consuming and appear less than credible. In the case of some talent practices, either the CEO believes that it is the right thing to do or he does not. If he does not, you will want to leverage practices that have a more measurable return or consider the alternate approaches that we discuss next.

Personal Appeal

According to Kevin Cox of American Express, "Leadership often fails to remember the interventions, learnings, and development opportunities that helped them to achieve their potential." The personal appeal requires that we gently remind them. We can each reflect on our careers and identify one or two powerful developmental experiences. Unless these were painful (and sometimes even if they were), we likely feel that some variant of that experience would also benefit other leaders. Use these experiences to your advantage when trying to convince reluctant executives to support a program or process. Did they have an overseas assignment that they felt was critical to their career? Use that fact to propose that more leaders get developmental assignments. Did they have a mentor whom they valued? Encourage the executive to share his wisdom with high-potential leaders so they will grow to be great leaders like him.

Competitive Appeal

Point out to hypercompetitive executives that the competition is leaving them in the dust: "Did you see that article in the *Journal* where CEO Smith talked about their talent reviews building better leaders than the competition?" Or "My friend in consulting said that she was teaching XYZ Corp's executives in a weekend leadership class! They seem pretty serious about growing their leaders quickly."

If you do not believe this tactic works, ask yourself how many companies have one or more corporate processes that they blindly copied from GE just because of its reputation. The only caution is that if your company has completely outflanked the competition, executives will not likely be impressed by what numbers two and three are doing.

You may have examples that work as well as these or better. The bottom line is that if the CEO or senior team doesn't "get" talent, it is your job to try to convey the facts. If, after repeated effort, you find they remain unconvinced, in all likelihood they are not going to get it, which suggests you are not in an environment conducive to long-term professional success. According to Lucien Alziari at Avon Products, "Life is too short to work with line leaders who at the most basic level don't have a talent mind-set."

Avoidance of Complexity Creep

Designing a simple, value-adding talent practice is a great start, but it is wasted effort if complexity creeps back in over time. Think of complexity as the natural state to which talent processes will return without constant vigilance—the metaphorical weeds in the talent management garden. Whether through well-intended changes in response to a client's request or a regional team adapting the process to local conditions, processes are always at risk. Effectively managing the propensity toward complexity requires regular monitoring of the processes and measuring their effectiveness. The best strategy includes conducting regular value-complexity audits, keeping process designs stable, and frequently measuring process outcomes.

Conduct Value-Complexity Audits

An annual value-complexity audit can ensure that any complexity that has crept into the process is found and eliminated. Even if your process design was once a masterpiece of OPTM, you may find that, over time, it requires more effort than expected or the level of value delivered does not meet original expectations. Something in the organization may have changed that allows you to remove even more complexity from the process.

In a value-complexity audit, you evaluate every element in a talent practice to ensure that the value added still outweighs the complexity created. The steps are simple:

- *Gather data about user satisfaction.* Ideally, this quantitative survey of managers who use the process asks about complexity, the value of the practice as a business tool, improvements they would like, and so on. You should also get input from HR leaders (via survey) about their perceptions of their line managers' satisfaction with the practice.

- *Inventory the practice.* Create a list of every design element included in a process and every action necessary to complete it. Review the survey data to see if there are other elements to add. List these elements in one column and create two columns next to it to evaluate each element's complexity and value (see table 7-1).

- *Conduct the audit.* Sitting with the HR or talent management team, review each element on the inventory list. Ask the team:

  - How can we make this step easier?

  - How can we make this step add more value?

  - If users are adding steps to the process, why is this happening?

  - If we eliminated this step or element, what percentage of people will care?

Using the Value-Complexity Curve as a guide, rate each element or step as continue, caution, or stop.

TABLE 7-1

Performance Management Value-Complexity Audit

Element or step	Can we remove complexity?	Can we add value?	Continue, caution, or stop
Goal box	No		Continue
Metric box	Yes. Instructions above box are more complex than needed.		Continue
Required quarterly review	Yes. No proven benefit to quarterly review.		Caution
Manager checks if employee has electronically acknowledged review.		Yes. Have e-mail sent to manager listing status of each employee with a link that can be clicked to send a reminder e-mail.	Continue
...	...	...	...

Maintain Design Stability

Even if the process changes eliminate complexity or add value, managers do not want the process to seem new each time they use it. The audit may show complexity is creeping in, but be careful to adjust the process in a way that is seamless to its users. Required fundamental changes should take place at about three-year intervals. Subtle process adjustments should take place no more than once a year.

Measure Process Outcomes

A talent practice is not working if the key metrics are not moving in the right direction. For each talent practice, identify one or two metrics that show if a process is delivering the expected business results. This is different than a metric that tells you if the process itself is working (e.g., measuring the participation rate on the employee survey). For example, if the objective is to increase the alignment between the organization's strategic goals and employees' actions, the metrics could be how many employees feel their goals are related to the larger strategic goals (engagement survey measure)

What About Technology?

You may be surprised that you have read this entire book and we have not once mentioned talent management technology. We are not biased against HR technology. We think it has tremendous potential to enable OPTM practices. But we do have two serious concerns about how it is currently applied to talent management.

Our first concern is that most talent management software designers commit the same error as the camera designers we discussed in the preface. They have included every possible bell and whistle in their systems. This conflicts with the simplicity and ease-of-use approach that is at the heart of OPTM. Software vendors explain that those features can all be turned off to make the process simpler, but that often constrains the required functionality, resulting in greater complexity as trade-off decisions are made. It also becomes more challenging to rein in business and HR leaders who are tempted by the bells and whistles and point out that the organization is already paying for them.

Our second concern is that we hear far too many talent managers answer the question, "What's your process for [performance management/talent reviews/development planning]?" with the name of a software program. "We use TalentTech for performance management" says nothing about what your process is or should be. Talent processes should never be defined by software. Software should enable the talent practices. The ideal talent management software enables managers to more easily execute simple processes or provides data that supports smarter decisions on business and people.

and an assessment of how many goals are truly aligned in this way (performance goal audit). A measure of how many midyear reviews were held does not answer the question.

The Right Talent for Talent Management

The largest driver of sustainability is the capability of the talent managers. We have heard equally strong cases that HR leaders should run talent management or that specialist talent management leaders are best suited for the job. Regardless of the structure or the job title, these leaders must have functional expertise, business knowledge, and strong influencing skills to be truly effective.

The challenge in finding talent management capability is that many HR professionals have experience in employee relations, recruiting, or organization development, but limited perspective on business operations. Although functional knowledge is valuable, the ability to influence a reluctant business executive on talent decisions requires a business mind-set. In addition to their functional skills, talent management leaders must know and love business, have a production mind-set, and display courage.

Know and Love Business

Talent managers must understand the financial, operational, and strategic realities of business, in general, and their organization's business, in particular. They should be able to address the challenges and opportunities in their business environment with as much fact-based knowledge as any other business leader.

Know the business. At a minimum, people managing talent-building processes should have business literacy that includes an ability to understand company financial statements, basic knowledge of how a good or service is produced, and operative knowledge of one of the classic strategy models at a minimum acceptable level. Ideally, they can pull apart a balance sheet, understand the drivers behind the company's brand strength, know the layout of the factories, and describe the intricacies of the supply chain. Jim Shanley, formerly of Bank of America, has a metric for an effective talent management or HR professional. If you walk into a room where the CEO, the CFO, and the head of talent management are talking business, you should not know which one is the talent management leader.

Love the business. Leaders involved in talent management should have a deep and abiding curiosity about how business works. They should love new product creation, the selling process, the journey from raw material to finished product, and the constant struggle to satisfy the customer. This quality is highly intangible, but has a meaningful impact on effectiveness.

Have a Production Mind-Set

Those in talent management often see their role as craftsmen—individuals tasked with carving special and unique leaders, one by one. Many in the field are challenged by the thought that they should treat the production of leaders like the production of widgets. The reality is that talent management is a production job, and they are the plant managers of the talent factory. Talent managers need to ensure that the raw material is in place, the production line is moving at an appropriate speed, and the stamping, cutting, and polishing machines are each working properly. At the end of the line, they need to guarantee that the product matches their customer's specifications and that they retool any products that do not.

Display Courage

The greatest challenge for a talent manager or HR leader implementing OPTM is avoiding the complexity creep discussed in the preface. A short time after the launch of OPTM practices, a line or HR leader will likely approach you with a simple request: "We love that new performance management process. Thanks for making it so easy. What would be really helpful is if you could just add ..." This will be the first test of how sustainable OPTM will be in your organization. Minor adjustments based on customers' feedback may be fine, but anything beyond that puts you a full step onto the slippery slope toward complexity. Will you be able to refuse the next request when you made changes for others?

Your choice is to stick to your convictions—that simple, robust processes always work best—or to compromise a little and hope that it is the last time. Of course, feedback from internal clients on usability and value are at the heart of the OPTM approach, but the courage to stand behind simplified process until there has been sufficient time to assess the impact is critical.

Conclusion

We know that today's talent practices are not meeting executives' needs. Executives are concerned about their organization's lack of talent and doubtful that the capability exists to produce more. Even with the answers on how to grow talent readily available, they do not see that knowledge translating into results. We believe the solution lies in radically simplifying and adding value to talent management practices to ensure their implementation and release their scientifically proven power. By adding transparency and accountability to those practices, we can ensure that they operate smoothly and sustainably.

Your journey to OPTM will be challenging. Those with a vested interest in the status quo will object to your ideas. Those who are simply afraid of change will insist that things are "good enough." Given the status of talent in organizations, however, you face a clear choice. Your organization can continue to repeat the same talent practices while hoping for a different outcome. Or it can commit to a sustainable new approach for building better talent faster.

NOTES

Preface

1. James Surowiecki, "Feature Presentation," *New Yorker*, May 28, 2007, http://www.newyorker.com/talk/financial/2007/05/28/070528ta_talk_surowiecki?printable=true.

2. Marc Effron, Shelly Greenslade, and Michelle Salob, *Top Companies for Leaders 2005* (Lincolnshire, IL: Hewitt Associates LLC, 2005).

3. New Talent Management Network, "Second Annual Talent Management Survey," January 2009, http://www.newtmn.com/includes/documents/2nd_annual_NTMN_Survey.pdf.

Chapter 1

1. Deloitte Touche Tohmatsu and the Economist Intelligence Unit, *Aligned at the Top: How Business and HR Executives View Today's Most Significant People Challenges—and What They're Doing About It* (New York: Deloitte Touche Tohmatsu, May 2007), 6; Ranier Strack, Jean-Michel Caye, Michael Leicht, Ulrich Villis, Hans Böhm, and Michael McDonnell, *The Future of HR in Europe: Key Challenges Through 2015* (Boston: Boston Consulting Group, June 2007), 16; Matthew Guthridge, Aamus Komm, and Emily Lawson, "Making Talent a Strategic Priority," *McKinsey Quarterly*, no. 1 (2008): 50–59.

2. Marc Effron, Shelly Greenslade, and Michelle Salob, *Top Companies for Leaders 2005* (Lincolnshire, IL: Hewitt Associates LLC, 2005); Mark Huselid, Susan Jackson, and Randall Schuler, "Technical and Strategic Human Resources Management Effectiveness as Determinants of Firm Performance," *Academy of Management Journal* 40, no. 1 (February 1997): 171–188, AOM Archive, Ebscohost.

3. Avon Products, Inc., "The Avon Opportunity, Annual Report 2007," http://www.avoncompany.com/investor/annualreport/pdf/annualreport2008.pdf, October 8, 2009.

4. Michael Lominger and Robert Eichinger, *The Leadership Machine: Architecture to Develop Leaders for Any Future* (Minneapolis, MN: Lominger International, 2002).

Chapter 2

1. Elaine Pulakos, *A Roadmap for Developing, Implementing, and Evaluating Performance Management Systems* (Alexandria, VA: SHRM Foundation, 2004).

2. "Chronology of Employee Performance Management in the Federal Government," February 23, 2009, http://www.opm.gov/perform/chron.asp.

3. Edwin Locke and Gary Latham, *A Theory of Goal Setting and Task Performance* (Englewood Cliffs, NJ: Prentice Hall, 1990); Victor Vroom, *Work and Motivation* (New York: John Wiley and Sons, 1964).

4. Locke and Latham, *A Theory of Goal Setting and Task Performance.*

5. Vroom, *Work and Motivation.*

6. Locke and Latham, *A Theory of Goal Setting and Task Performance.*

7. Daniel Simons and Christopher Chabris, "Gorillas in Our Midst: Sustained Inattentional Blindness for Dynamic Events," *Perception* 28 (1999): 1059–1074.

8. Lisa Ordoñez, Maurice Scheitzer, Adam Galinsky, and Max Bazerman, "Goals Gone Wild: The Systematic Side Effects of Overprescribing Goal Setting," *Academy of Management Perspectives* 23, no. 1 (February 2009): 6–16.

9. Mandy Cheng, Peter Luckett, and Habib Mahama, "Effect of Perceived Conflict Among Multiple Performance Goals and Goal Difficulty on Task Performance," *Accounting and Finance* 47, no. 2 (2007): 221–242.

10. Edwin Locke, Ken Smith, Miriam Erez, Dong-Ok Chah, and Adam Schaffer, "The Effect of Intra-Individual Goal Conflict on Performance," *Journal of Management* 20 (1994): 67–91.

11. Miriam Erez and R. Arad, "Participative Goal Setting, Motivational and Cognitive Factors," *Journal of Applied Psychology* 71 (1986): 591–597.

12. Gary Latham, Miriam Erez, and Edwin Locke, "Resolving Scientific Disputes by the Joint Design of Crucial Experiments by the Antagonists: Application to the Erez-Latham Dispute Regarding Participation in Goal Setting," *Journal of Applied Psychology* 73 (1988): 753–772.

13. Steven Scullen, Paul Bergey, and Lynda Aiman-Smith, "Forced Distribution Rating Systems and the Improvement of Workforce Potential: A Baseline Simulation," *Personnel Pscyhology* 58, no.1 (2005), 1–32.

14. Frank Landy and James Farr, "Performance Rating," *Psychological Bulletin* 876, no. 1 (1980): 72–107.

15. Paul Kingstrom and Alan Bass, "A Critical Analysis of Studies Comparing Behaviorally Anchored Rating Scales (BARS) and Other Rating Formats," *Personnel Psychology* 34, no. 9 (2006): 263–289.

16. Robert Bretz, George Milkovich, and Walter Read, "The Current State of Performance Appraisal Research and Practice: Concerns, Directions, and Implications," *Journal of Management* 18 (1992): 321–352.

17. Anne Tsui and Patricia Ohlott, "Multiple Assessment of Managerial Effectiveness: Interrater Agreement and Consensus in Effectiveness Models," *Personnel Psychology* 41 (1988): 779–803.

Chapter 3

1. Gary Latham and Edward Locke, "Self-regulation Through Goal Setting," *Organizational Behavior and Human Decision Processes* 50 (1991): 212–247, p. 224; Gina Toegel and Jay Conger, "360°-Degree Assessment: Time for Reinvention," *Academy of Management Learning and Education* 2, no. 3 (2003): 297–311.

2. Robert Ammons, "Effects of Knowledge of Performance: A Survey and Tentative Theoretical Formulation," *Journal of General Psychology* 54, (1956): 279–299.

3. Avraham Kluger and Angelo DeNisi, "The Effects of Feedback Interventions on Performance: A Historical Review, a Meta-Analysis, and a Preliminary Feedback Intervention Theory," *Psychological Bulletin* 119, (1996): 254–284.

4. Ibid.

5. Ibid.

6. James Smither, Joan Brett, and Leanne Atwater, "What Do Leaders Recall About Their Multisource Feedback?" *Journal of Leadership & Organizational Studies* 14, no. 3 (2008): 202–218.

7. Ibid.

8. Marshall Goldsmith and Howard Morgan, "Leadership Is a Contact Sport," *Strategy + Business*, August 2004, 71–79.

9. Marshall Goldsmith, "Leadership Development: Try Feedforward Instead of Feedback," *Journal for Quality and Participation* 26, no. 3 (2003): 38–42.

10. Anne Tsui and Patricia Ohlott, "Multiple Assessment of Managerial Effectiveness: Interrater Agreement and Consensus in Effectiveness Models," *Personnel Psychology* 41, no. 4 (1988): 779–803.

11. Manuel London and J. Smither, "Can Multi-Source Feedback Change Perceptions of Goal Accomplishment, Self-Evaluations, and Performance Related Outcomes?" *Personnel Psychology* 48, no. 4 (1995): 803–839.

Chapter 4

1. Marc Effron, Shelly Greenslade, and Michelle Salob, *Top Companies for Leaders 2005* (Lincolnshire, IL: Hewitt Associates LLC, 2005).

2. Wei Shen and Albert Cannella Jr., "Revisiting the Performance Consequences of CEO Succession: The Impact of Successor Type, Post-succession Senior Executive Turnover, and Departing CEO Tenure," *Academy of Management Journal* 45, no. 4 (2002): 717–733.

3. Leaetta Hough and Frederick Oswald, "Personnel Selection: Looking Towards the Future—Remembering the Past," *Annual Review of Psychology* 51 (February 2000): 631–664.

4. Frank Schmidt and John Hunter, "General Mental Ability in the World of Work: Occupational Attainment and Job Performance," *Journal of Personality and Social Psychology* 86, no. 1 (2004): 162–173.

5. Ibid.

6. Ibid.

7. Philip Bobko, Philip Roth, and Denise Potosky, "Derivation and Implications of a Meta-Analytic Matrix Incorporating Cognitive Ability, Alternative Predictors, and Job Performance," *Personnel Psychology* 52, no. 3 (1999): 561–589.

8. Deniz Ones, Stephan Dilcerht, Chockalingam Viswesvaran, and Timothy Judge, "In Support of Personality Assessment in Organization Settings," *Personnel Psychology* 60, no. 4 (2007): 995–1027.

9. Michael Mount and Murray Barrick, "The Big Five Personality Dimensions: Implications for Research and Practice in Human Resource Management," *Research in Personnel and Human Resource Management* 13 (1995): 153–200.

10. Charles O'Reilly III, Jennifer Chatman, and David Caldwell, "People and Organizational Culture: A Profile Comparison Approach to Assessing Person-Organization Fit," *Academy of Management Journal* 34, no. 3 (September 1991): 487–516.

11. Marc Effron, Shelly Greenslade, and Michelle Salob, *Top Companies for Leaders 2005* (Lincolnshire, IL: Hewitt Associates LLC, 2005).

12. Ibid.

Chapter 5

1. John Thackray, "Feedback for Real," *Gallup Management Journal*, March 3, 2001, http://gmj.gallup.com.

2. Anthony J. Rucci, Steven P. Kirn, and Richard T. Quinn, "The Employee-Customer-Profit Chain at Sears," *Harvard Business Review*, January-February 1998, 82–97.

3. Towers Perrin, *Closing the Engagement Gap: A Roadmap for Driving Superior Business Results* (Stamford, CT: *Global Workforce Study*: Towers Perrin, 2009).

4. Bryan Ott, "Investors, Take Note: Engagement Boosts Earnings," Release Date: 6/14/2007, http://gmj.gallup.com.

5. John Gibbons, *Employee Engagement: A Review of Current Research and Its Implications* (New York: Conference Board, 2006).

6. Wilmar Schaufeli, Marissa Salanova, Vincente Gonzalez-Roma, and Arnold Bakker, "The Measurement of Engagement and Burnout: A Two Sample Confirmatory Factor Analytic Approach," *Journal of Happiness Studies* 3, no. 1 (2002): 71–92.

7. James Harter and Frank Schmidt, "Conceptual Versus Empirical Distinctions Among Constructs: Implications for Discriminant Validity," *Industrial and Organizational Psychology* 1, no. 1 (2008): 36–39.

8. Frederick Herzberg, Bernard Mausner, and Barbara Block Snyderman, *The Motivation to Work* (New York: John Wiley, 1959).

9. Richard Hackman and Greg Oldham, "Development of the Job Diagnostic Survey," *Journal of Applied Psychology* 60, no. 2 (April 1975): 159–170.

10. Tally Dvir, Dov Eden, Bruce Avolio, and Boas Shamir, "Impact of Transformational Leadership on Follower Development and Performance: A Field Study," *Academy of Management Journal* 45, no. 4 (2002): 735–744.

11. Linda Rhoades and Robert Eisenberger, "Perceived Organizational Support: A Review of the Literature," *Journal of Applied Psychology* 87, no. 4 (2002): 698–714.

12. Jay Conger, Jay Alden, and Rabindra Kanungo, "Charismatic Leadership in Organizations: Perceived Behavioral Attributes and Their Measurement," *Journal of Organizational Behavior* 15, no. 5 (September 1994): 439–452.

13. William Macey and Benjamin Schneider, "The Meaning of Employee Engagement," *Industrial and Organizational Psychology: Perspectives on Science and Practice* 1, no. 1 (2008): 3–30.

14. Ibid.

15. James Harter, Frank Schmidt, and Theodore Hayes, "Business-Unit-Level Relationship Between Employee Satisfaction, Employee Engagement, and Business Outcomes: A Meta-Analysis," *Journal of Applied Psychology* 87, no. 2 (2002): 268–279.

16. Towers Perrin, *Closing the Engagement Gap: A Roadmap for Driving Superior Business Results* (Stamford, CT: Towers Perrin, Global Workforce Study, 2009).

17. Gibbons, *Employee Engagement.*

18. Reanna Poncheri, Jennifer Lindberg, Lori Foster Thompson, and Eric Surface, "A Comment on Employee Surveys: Negativity Bias in Open Ended Responses," *Organizational Research Methods* 11, no. 3 (July 2008): 614–630.

19. Jon Krosnick, "Survey Research," *Annual Review of Psychology* 50 (February 1999): 537–567.

Chapter 6

1. Marc Effron, Shelly Greenslade, and Michelle Salob, *Top Companies for Leaders 2005* (Lincolnshire, IL: Hewitt Associates LLC, 2005).

2. David McClelland, "Testing for Competence Rather Than for 'Intelligence,'" *American Psychologist* 28, no. 1 (1973): 1–14.

3. Signe Spencer and Lyle Spencer, *Competence at Work* (New York: John Wiley, 1973).

4. Paul Sparrow, "Organisational Competencies: A Valid Approach for the Future?" and "A Rejoinder to Anderson and Iles," *International Journal of Selection and Assessment* 3, no. 3 (1995): 168–177 and 202–204.

5. McClelland, "Testing for Competence Rather Than for 'Intelligence.'"

6. Tom Cockerill, John Hunt, and Harry Schroder, "Managerial Competencies: Fact or Fiction?" *Business Strategy Review* 6, no. 3 (Autumn 1995): 1–12.

7. Gerald Barrett and Robert Depinet, "A Reconsideration of Testing for Competence Rather Than Intelligence," *American Psychologist* 46, no. 10 (1991): 101–124; Edward Lawler, "Competencies: The Right Foundation for the New Pay?" *CEO Publication G96-3 (297)*, Center for Effective Organizations, April 1996, http://ceo.usc.edu/pdf/G963297.pdf.

8. Jeffery Schippmann, Garry Hughes, and Erich Prien, "The Use of Structured Multidomain Job Analysis for the Construction of Assessment Center Methods and Procedure," *Journal of Business and Psychology* 1, no. 4 (1987): 353–366.

9. Randall Peterson, D. Brent Smith, Paul Martorana, and Pamela Owens, "The Impact of Chief Executive Officer Personality on Top Management Team Dynamics: One Mechanism by Which Leadership Affects Organizational Performance," *Journal of Applied Psychology* 88, no. 5 (2003): 795–808.

10. James Harter, Frank Schmidt, and Theodore Hayes, "Business-Unit-Level Relationship Between Employee Satisfaction, Employee Engagement, and Business Outcomes: A Meta-Analysis," *Journal of Applied Psychology* 87, no. 2 (2002): 268–279.

11. Richard Boyatzis, "Competencies in the 21st Century," *Journal of Management Development* 27, no. 1 (2008): 5–12.

12. Gary Hamel and C. K. Prahalad, "Core Competence of the Corporation," *Harvard Business Review*, May–June 1990, 79–91.

13. Towers Perrin, *Pulse Survey Report: Managing Talent in Tough Times,* Towers Perrin, October 2009, http://www.towersperrin.com/tp/getwebcachedoc?webc=USA/2009/200909/Managing_Talent_Pulse_Survey_9-29-09.pdf; Marc Effron and Richard Wellins, *2009 State of Talent Management Survey*, New Talent Management Network, January 2009, http://www.newtmn.com/survey.php.

14. Effron and Wellins, *2009 State of Talent Management Survey*.

15. Leanne Markus, Helena Cooper-Thomas, and Keith Allpress, "Confounded by Competencies? An Evaluation of the Evolution and Use of Competency Models," *New Zealand Journal of Psychology* 34, no. 2 (July 2005): 117–126.

16. Amy Kristof-Brown, Ryan Zimmerman, and Erin Johnson, "Consequences of an Individuals' Fit at Work: A Meta-Analysis of Person-Job, Person-Organization, Person-Group, and Person-Supervisor Fit," *Personnel Psychology* 58, no. 2 (2005): 281–342.

17. Michael Porter, *On Competition* (Boston: Harvard Business School Press, 1998).

18. Jay Barney, "Firm Resources and Sustained Competitive Advantage," *Journal of Management* 17, no. 1 (1991): 99–120.

19. Robert Quinn and Kim Cameron, "Organizational Life Cycles and Shifting Criteria of Effectiveness: Some Preliminary Evidence," *Management Science* 29, no. 1 (January 1983): 33–51.

20. Noel Tichy and Mary Anne Devanna, *The Transformational Leader* (New York: John Wiley, 1986).

21. Anisya Thomas, Robert Litscher, and Kanan Ramaswamy, "The Performance Impact of Strategy-Manager Coalignment: An Empirical Study," *Strategic Management Journal* 12, no. 7 (1991): 509–522.

INDEX

ABOUT THE AUTHORS

MARC EFFRON helps companies build better talent faster.

Marc is President of the Talent Strategy Group, a full-service talent management consultancy. As a talent management leader, Marc has worked for and consulted to some of the world's largest and most successful companies. He applies a simplicity-based approach to building talent that emphasizes transparency and managerial accountability.

In addition to writing *One Page Talent Management*, Marc coauthored *Leading the Way* (2004), coedited *Human Resources in the 21st Century* (2001), and has written chapters in nine management and leadership books. He has created leading-edge research on talent issues, including the iconic "Top Companies for Leaders" study and the New Talent Management Network's annual "State of Talent Management" survey.

He is widely quoted in the business media, is a sought-after speaker, and was recently named as one of the Top 100 Influencers in HR. He earned an MBA with honors letters from the Yale School of Management and a BA in political science from the University of Washington.

Marc's prior experience includes serving as Vice President, Global Talent Management, for Avon Products; and starting and leading the Global Leadership Consulting Practice at Hewitt Associates. He was also Senior Vice President, Leadership Development, for Bank of America; Director of Organization Effectiveness and Learning for Oxford Health Plans; and a compensation consultant for a global consulting firm. Marc previously served as a political consultant and a congressional staff assistant.

In 2007, Marc founded the New Talent Management Network (http://www.newtmn.com/), a nonprofit networking and research organization focused on increasing the effectiveness of talent management practitioners. It is now the world's largest talent management organization, with more than eighteen hundred members.

He can be reached at marc@talentstrategygroup.com. More information is available at www.talentstrategygroup.com.

MIRIAM ORT has held leadership positions in talent management and human resources in the HR organizations of *Fortune* 500 companies. She is a frequent contributor to publications on leadership and talent management, and has spoken on the topic at industry events such as International Consortium for Executive Development Resources (ICEDR) and Society for Industrial Organizational Psychology (SIOP).

Miriam is currently a senior human resources manager at PepsiCo. She codeveloped the One Page Talent Management approach while at Avon Products, where she most recently led the talent management area for Avon Products North America. In that role, her responsibilities included performance management, leadership development, and talent planning for over six thousand associates. She also codesigned many of the talent management practices being used globally at Avon. Her previous experience includes workforce analytics, compensation, and HR generalist roles.

Miriam also coauthored "Talent Pool or Talent Puddle?" in the *AMA Handbook of Leadership* (2010) and has appeared as a blog contributor for *Harvard Business Review* online. She holds an MA in human resources management from Rutgers University and a BA in English from Thomas Edison State College.